Deliberate Performance

A Pragmatic Approach to Strategy and Execution in the Modern Economy

Printed in the United States of America

First Printing, 2016

ISBN 978-0-9975035-0-0

Folino Media
64 Blazier Road
Martinsville NJ 08836

www.FolinoMedia.com

For my Mother and Father.

Table of Contents

FORWARD

This brief book is about improving organizational performance in an increasingly complex, disruptive, and hyper competitive environment through deliberate focus on key, interlinked, management decisions and actions. Prior to unpacking that statement and getting to the core content, I think it's helpful to chart the territory out at a high level to get one's bearings.

Semantics

For consistency, I will use *enterprise* to talk about the entirety of the business and use *organization* to talk about a functional business unit. They can be one and the same or there can be multiple organizations within an enterprise. But the reasons for the distinction will be made clear later on.

Organizational performance scope here involves both tactical and strategic dimensions: in the former, how to operationally execute — meaning choices in resources, process, culture and innovation focus resulting from the *operating strategy*; in the latter, selecting the intent, market, and how one chooses to compete (more traditional domains of strategy).

Themes

Four themes drive this book. My intent at this point is neither to argue nor unpack them — rather simply bring them to the reader's attention.

1. **Apply** Networked Competencies as an approach to understand markets, strategic objectives and operating strategies.
2. **Distribute and align** decisions across the organization to drive performance through both a *narrative framework* and a robust *information architecture.*
3. **Clarify purpose and strategic objectives and align** resources, processes, culture and innovation investments — all of which drive decisioning — accordingly to drive performance.
4. **Review, revisit, adjust** the enterprise's structure and enterprise-level resources, processes and culture in light of the new environment (particularly for incumbent enterprises).

Approach

The below picture summarizes the core approach of this book. As in Themes above, detailing the concepts is the subject of the rest of this book. For this forward section, the intent is awareness.

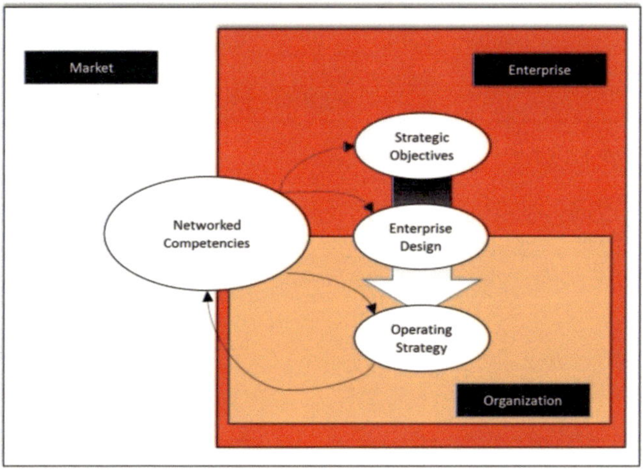

To break the picture down, there are three domains (in increasing level of specificity): market[1], enterprise, and organization.

[1] I am mindful of the slipperiness of 'market' and will address same in Part I (Networked Competencies).

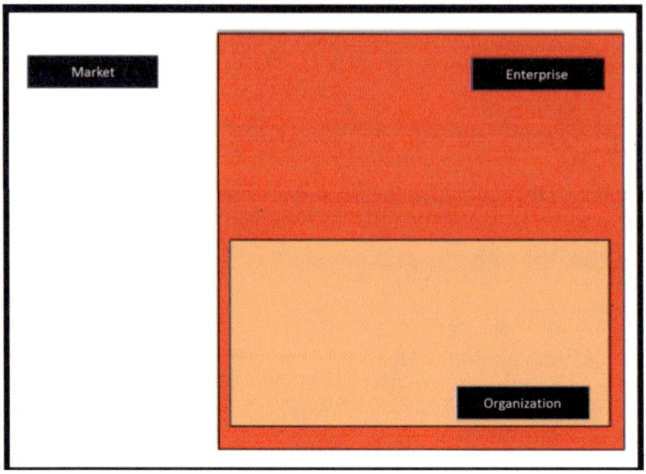

Networked Competencies approach (covered in Part I) creates a lens with which to view the market, how one is competing, developments, etc. and touches all the domains.

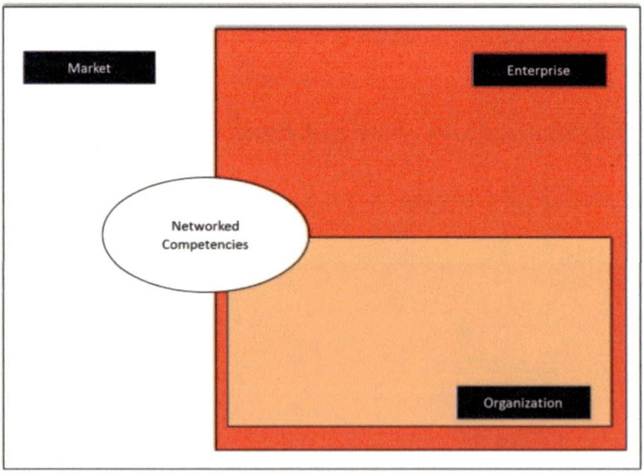

Strategic Objectives, Enterprise Design and Operating Strategy (covered in Parts II through IV) are the generally sequential steps of management from the 'What' (structurally) to the 'How' (structural and tactical).

The final links come from (a) Networked Competencies informing the Strategic Objectives process and (b) resources, processes, culture, and innovation focus resulting from Operating Strategy inform further Networked Competencies reviews.

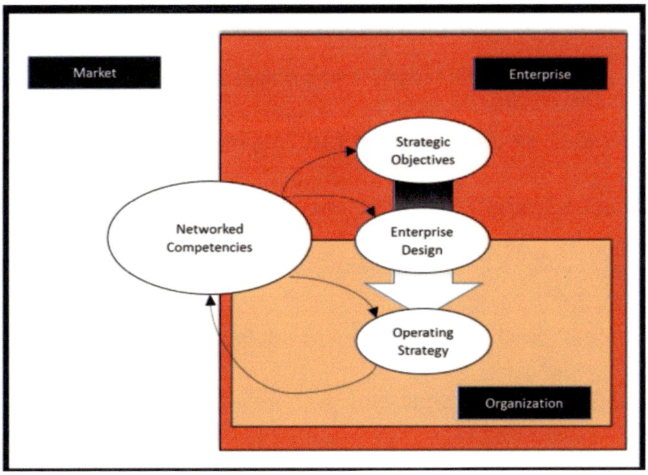

Moving beyond the approach framework, a few comments about the narrative approach.

- *Systemic* — in that it applies theory and practice, strategy and execution as well as people, process and technology for a wide angled lens to identify the relevant aspects to consider and key dynamics driving change into the system.
- *Pragmatic* — the approach described herein is unapologetically mired in messy, pragmatic, aspects of strategy. 'Strategic thinking' suffers from being synonymous with big picture decision-making while not having to deal with burdensome details. Successful outcomes of strategy require a more pragmatic view involving deliberate selection / deselection of objectives and process. To effectively understand what to select or deselect requires engaging and clarifying data and (a) selecting what needs to be acted on now, (b) deselecting but cataloguing for later reference and (c) deselecting and moving on. Process involves both acknowledging an organization as being constructed of people and therefore factor in the tasks of alignment and deliberate practice and, like every other process, strategy has defined outputs, critical success factors and milestones.
- *Dense* — specificity and detail while avoiding jargon — unless explicitly defined, at which point it becomes short-hand.

INTRODUCTION

My intent here is to identify key narrative strands highlighting challenges facing today's organizations and suggest that a new approach is required.

Complexity & Unpredictability

Wikipedia's July 2015 entry on Complexity states it "is generally used to characterize something with many parts where those parts interact with each other in multiple ways."

More importantly, in business, complexity makes it not simply *hard* to accurately anticipate but *impossible* to anticipate given the number of contributing factors and uncertainties up-front, coupled with second order effects and iterative adjustments made by market players.

Just to walk through one simple narrative — retail buying — a few years into the e-commerce adoption cycle, where consumers now expect purchasing platforms to support omni-channel purchasing (physical brick & mortar stores, web, mobile). Product availability isn't as much a concern with all the options, so now differentiating considerations in consumer behaviors shift to:

- Experience — with product presumed available, people can spend time doing things that hit personal dopamine triggers: perhaps enjoying the treasure-hunt-surprises at HomeGoods or Tuesday Morning, coveting new technologies at Best Buy or Apple, working with a personal shopper / partner at Nordstrom to work through modern and classic looks, or sifting through the produce and ingredients at the market to plan Saturday's meal.
- Convenience — the flip side of Experience is that one doesn't need to spend considerable time doing what one doesn't want - or have the time - to do. Not sure about size and don't want the store / dressing room experience? Order three and return the two that don't fit. Don't want to do the groceries? Order and pick them up or have them delivered.
- Contexts — 'mobile' from the corporate IT point of view is a technical platform but it represents very different contexts (e.g., time-wasting-browsing-waiting-in-line, comparison-shopping-while-browsing-stores or oh-just-need-to-pick-this-up-while-on-the-way-home) — each of

which present different opportunities to retailers and potential distribution points and should be handled differently. This context-centric view extends beyond mobile across all purchasing channels.

- Personal Association — what else will make me feel good about my purchase? Buying from a company who represents or supports a cause I support. Or to be 'cool' or 'different' - which can mean look - or not look - like something.
- Impulse — see something you like on YouTube or Netflix? Instagram? Pinterest? Facebook? Buy it now. May be something you never thought you needed, but seeing that particular celebrity on the hoverboard makes it worth buying.
- Changing values — share and re-use vs own? Maker movement and importance of crafting vs buying? Have we reached 'peak consumption'?

Retailers react via several paths:

- Status Quo — choose not to react. Dig in the heels. Resist change. In all likelihood, fail.
- Invest — develop new channels to catch-up with expectations established by leaders such as Amazon and Zappos.

- Optimize — apply established process disciplines to this new environment. For example, identify and implement cost management / reduction opportunities relevant to the new technology (e.g., ship from closest warehouse inventory, focusing on cartonization processes).
- Monitor evolving competitive landscape. Web-as-a-channel eliminates a number of distribution-related barriers to entry: a simply well-placed, potentially planned or coincidental advert (e.g., worn by Taylor Swift on a New York street or Ron Wood at a Hyde Park concert) or article regarding "The Best Hoodie Ever Made" can easily translate to purchases without a physical store front; manufacturers can go directly to the consumer via a web site and social media; retailers also need to consider potential influence of hardware players (as they own the device — phone, car, etc. - that interfaces with customer), software / ecosystem players such as Apple and Google, and social media tools such as Pinterest and Instagram (who are, not surprisingly, building "Buy It Now" like capabilities).

Amid all this are the demands of the current business which, inconveniently, don't subside. There is a tremendous investment and mindset rooted in legacy resources, processes, culture and innovation focus in which constituents have a significant stake. As in Professor Clay Christiansen's Disruption Model, legacy characteristics can work against the retailer at these points.

Putting all the standard demographic, international, economic meta-trends aside for the moment and consider just future IT waves:

- 3D additive printing. If you can design it — or download the design — you can make it. The need for a toys won't change but how they are created / delivered could drastically change (thereby potentially also affecting how raw materials are distributed).
- User Interface development — sensors, gestures and haptics (using touch / tactile sensations to interact with applications and systems). You create data while standing still - where your eyes go, how fast your heart beats, blood sugar levels, etc. Monitor that over time - with what you have done or eaten as context and it gets more interesting. Add active interaction or response to movements and gestures and it gets more complex.
- Augmented reality. Using technology to bring additional information to a situation. Google Glass perhaps wasn't a success in its first introduction, but being able to bring relevant information (best pricing, fit, recommended looks, narrative about manufacturer) could change the picture.

- Immersive reality. Like jet packs, virtual reality always seems to be on horizon. But the ability to provide feedback to your senses (visual and audio in virtual reality but additionally touch, temperature, smell, taste ...) could impact breadth and depth of experience opportunities.

Each of these would affect retailing in some form, but my point here isn't about futurism nor specifically retail — rather it's using a very simplified discussion to illustrate the technical, behavioral, economic and regulatory systems interacting to create complexity.

One could have a similar discussion in healthcare, finance, IT software & solutions and other sectors and points of view: different specifics and rates of change, perhaps, but IT — and more specifically the Internet, internationalization, regulatory environments and market pressures have combined to create that complexity.

Complexity brings uncertainty which, in turn, should be met by organizational clarity — meaning a clear, visible, shared, understanding of the organization's goals, process, roles / impact and data regarding external environment — and responsiveness — meaning the ability, through cultural values, structure, process, systems, to identify and adapt as necessitated — or not — by changes.

The future may be uncertain and organizations may or may not be positioned to shape it. But this does not eliminate organizations' responsibilities to decide, act and adjust (and, I hope, this is where this book can help).

Transaction Costs Shape the Organization

A brief detour into theory: back in 1937 in his "The Nature of the Firm," British and eventual Nobel Prize winning economist Ronald Coase argued that the relationship between transaction costs — which he defined as search and information costs, bargaining and decision costs, and policing and enforcement costs - and the scope of the firm, indicating a given firm's boundary will exist up to the point it organizes a transaction more efficiently than the market would.

While it omits certain pragmatics or behaviorals, the argument seems directionally sound: if an organization has the opportunity to reduce costs for processing accounts payable to a fraction of current cost levels through leveraging the market (i.e., outsourcing), all things otherwise being equal, they should.

I use Coase to ground this section although Christiansen's Value Chain Evolution (VCE) theory treads similar ground — highlighting how value chains move from integrated firms to more modular set-ups when enterprises can "*specify* their needs, *verify* the exchanges occurring are correct, and interactions across the interface should be *predictable*" (i.e., conditions with low transaction costs).[2]

Information technologies have gutted transaction costs, creating pressure to source more through market mechanisms — implying increased focus and specialization.

Cheaper and broader bandwidth, greatly simplified data standardization and integration, and a globally available platform in the Internet drastically cut costs associated with transactions: searching, qualifying, sourcing/contracting, interacting, monitoring, etc.

This process will continue as more capabilities are bolted onto the Internet platform: consider on-demand 3D printing and robotics that hint at making low-scale production as simple and efficient as submitting a plan or image.

Per Coase and applying Christiansen's assessment, these significant disruptions of transaction costs should change how firms are shaped — moving more

---

[2] Important also is Christiansen's point that integration may take precedent if there's a demonstrable performance improvement.

activities to be organized by the market (rather than internally) and, thereby, leading to specialization within the organization.[3]

Greater Consolidation + Increased Variability of Individual Firm Performance

Data for the United States shows increased consolidation across a number of sectors.

This structural change in concentration was recognized by the U.S. Department of Justice in 2010 when they raised the threshold of 'highly concentrated' as

---

[3] While emphasizing IT's impact in moving from in- to outsource, it's worth noting two counter-pressures. Neither, I think, changes the essential direction - but will influence the path.

- Increased connectedness and concern for information propriety creates direct costs (e.g., data security and compliance processes) and risks impacting how individual firms assess cost / benefits
- Information flow may not be equally distributed and symmetric - and these asymmetries will shape the competitive field. 'Siren servers' – using computer scientist, author and musician Jaron Lanier's language to describe high transaction players such as Google, Amazon, or Facebook - aggregate and can create significant value from high customer interaction and the capability to capture, store, recall, application and distribution data related to people's information (virtual, physical, biological). At the current time, the tools and structure to address the asymmetry are lacking and could shape the competitive field as players seek to control access to information and potential proprietary value and as an inflection point as individuals' right to their data (as an extension of self) is further qualified.

measured by the Herfindahl-Hirschman Index from 1800 to 2500 (these numbers, being the square of the enterprise's market share, equate to about 50% market share). However, the data (also depicted below) shows a significant increase over time.[4]

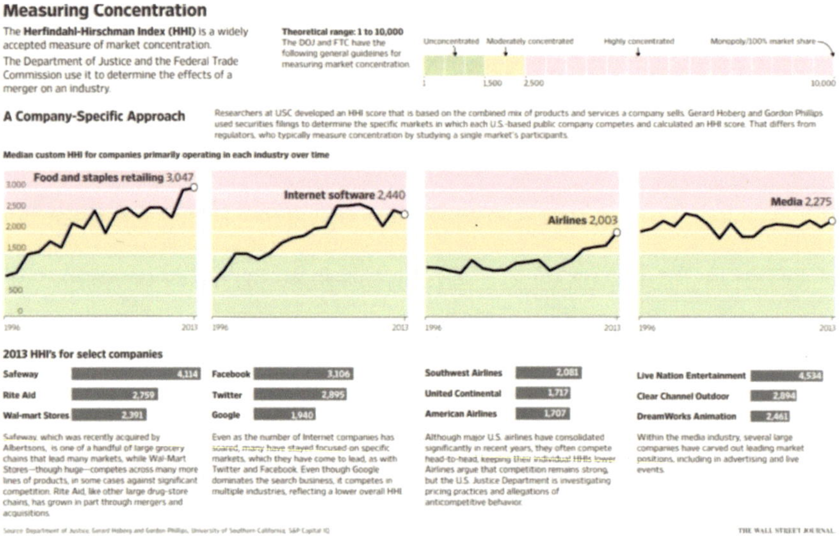

At the same time, the performance of individual firms has grown more volatile.

In their "The Rise of Firm-Level Volatility: Causes and Consequences," Diego Comin and Thomas Philippon documented that the frequency of companies dropping out of the top 20% in their sector more than doubled from 1990 to 2000.

---

[4] "Wave of Megadeals Tests Antitrust Limits in U.S." Wall Street Journal, October 18 2015

Separately, the below graphic from BCG Senior Partner and Managing Director Martin Reeves' "Your Strategy Needs a Strategy" highlights increased disparity between top and bottom performers — again emphasizing increased volatility and variability of performance.

Increasing gap between winners and losers for US companies

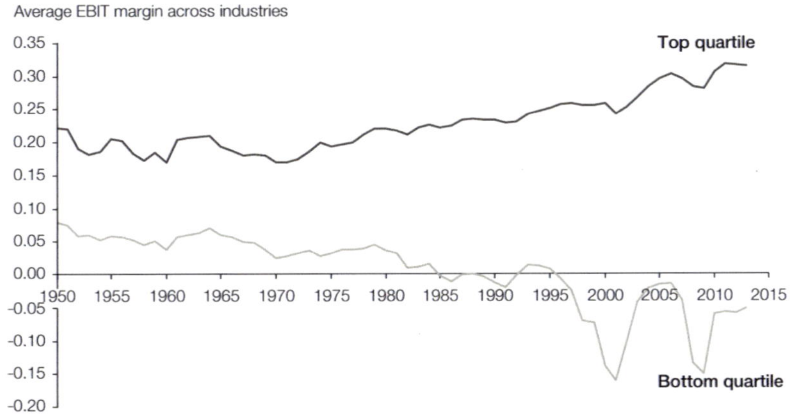

Source: BCG analysis (August 2014), Compustat.

Note: EBIT: earnings before interest and taxes. EBIT margin across industries is based on an analysis of approximately 34,000 publicly listed, mainly US companies in years when net sales were greater than $50 million; computing quartile average within six-digit GICS industry (unweighted), then averaged across industries (weighted by number of companies per industry per year); excluding outliers (higher than 100 percent margin or lower than minus 300 percent margin) and industries in years with insufficient data points.

The link here is not direct cause-and-effect but rather correlation.

Consolidation is sensible — almost irresistible: a defensive mechanism to drive bottom-line improvements through economies of scale and overhead cuts; in the world of top-line growth challenges, it's a low hanging opportunity.

The defensive mechanism doesn't address our current disruptive reality: where competition isn't like-for-like. The latter benefits the short run but kicks what seems to be the elephant-sized can (namely how to increase the top line) down the road.

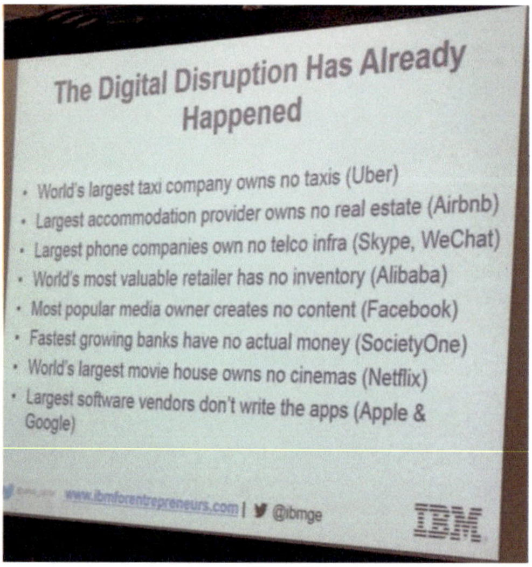

Path Forward

Each of these narratives — complexity yielding uncertainty, transaction costs shaping organizations, IT gutting transactions costs thereby driving increased focus into organizations and increased industry consolidation contemporaneous with increased variability of firm performance — points to a fundamental challenge facing today's enterprises.

And in facing these challenges, we need to look at the pragmatics of organizations and, specifically, the medium with which they operate.

Organizations are comprised of people and keeping tens, hundreds or thousands aligned with goals, focused on the 'right' things, engaged hopefully in constructive outcomes for the organization and avoiding tribalism, insular and dogmatic thinking is not easy and requires attention and its own considerations. Organizations are also an outcome of a series of both explicit and implicit decisions: investment in resources; processes instituted, practiced, and repeated; culture propagated over time; innovation focus reflecting how it changes over time. By design or by accident, an organization has developed — or been built — to do something.

Any discussion about organization performance that does not address these aspects is flawed.

Deliberate Performance

"Deliberate Performance" is both a method and a mindset.

The *method*, including both processes and key design tenets, are the core subject of this book and will follow the logical progression depicted below and described in the Forward.

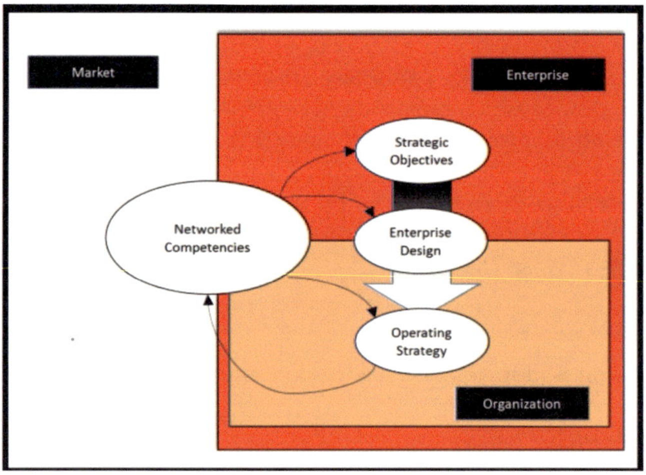

We start in Part I with the *Networked Competencies* methodology to describe how industries and markets are reshaping. It takes the form of a how-to process to develop your own Networked Competency map and, while doing so, describes the underlying key principles.

That market and the organization's current performance inform Part II — setting *Strategic Objectives*. Much of the focus here is on how value propositions are evolving and how organizations should react – it also touches on other key tenets in the strategic process such as selection and deselection.

Part III goes into *Enterprise Design* which speaks to how enterprises need to structure their efforts. If competencies and outcomes are aligned, the structure is simple and organization and enterprise are one and the same. However, if not aligned, then this part speaks to potential of *portfolio enterprises* and associated design principles.

Part IV shifts to *Operating Strategy* and the processes needed to drive decision distribution and alignment — focusing on setting and communicating performance narrative, information architecture and minding the culture.

Operating decisions drive organizations' resources-processes-culture-innovation focus, which in turn impacts relative market performance taking us back into the cycle and laying the foundation on which you continue to build.

Along the way of describing the method of *Deliberate Performance*, we will make a few, short digressions. They contribute to the themes of the book, demonstrate aspects of the method from alternate perspectives, but don't fit neatly into the narrative. I use the digression label and intentionally step out of the narrative to discuss pragmatic value of purpose, describe lily pad strategies, IT vendor selection and organizational transformation.

Mindset behind *Deliberate Performance* warrants brief, explicit, explanation.

- *Focus on what you can control.* The classic depiction of this is the archer who is instructed to focus on the processes of aiming at the target, drawing back the arrow and releasing it - and not to worry unduly on the outcome.

  In that vein, the method and tenets are almost exclusively centered on decisions and actions in management's hands.

- *Tapping information flows is in your control.* The classic archer depiction omits more modern elements potentially under her control such as planning, intelligence about environmental conditions and competition, feedback and even execution opportunities:
  - Obtain data regarding current and average conditions and previous shot results.
  - Receive real-time feedback regarding a previous shot (e.g., too far to the left) allowing compensation.

- Assess the most effective bows and arrows to be used for the given conditions.
- Can she shoot arrows twice as fast, effectively doubling probability of hitting the target.

This is why, for example, focused innovation and information flow play such critical roles in the method.

- *Be mindful - and constructively paranoid - of items outside your control.* For what you don't control, put in place reasonable processes and an information platform to learn what you can, take time out to learn known and unknown unknowns and pragmatically assess how that impacts your current and potentially future market.

  Deliberate Performance refers frequently to obtaining outside and additional inside perspectives to make better informed assessments and decisions.

  Echoing former Intel CEO Andy Grove's sentiment that "(c)omplacency breeds failure. Only the paranoid survive," [5] constructive paranoia drives innovation focus – which, as I will argue, sits at the core of

[5] Grove, Andrew. Only the Paranoid Survive, Doubleday (1996)

networked competencies (Part I) - and the importance of yin value proposition activities (see Part II).

- *'Think twice, then do.'* Create the space and rhythm to analyze and the need to take — or choose not to take — deliberate action. There is obviously a common sense balance to be struck regarding degree of analysis (i.e., more impactful decisions requiring more analysis) — but the need for both is critical.

With that, we now move to the core of the book and Networked Competencies.

PART I - NETWORKED COMPETENCIES

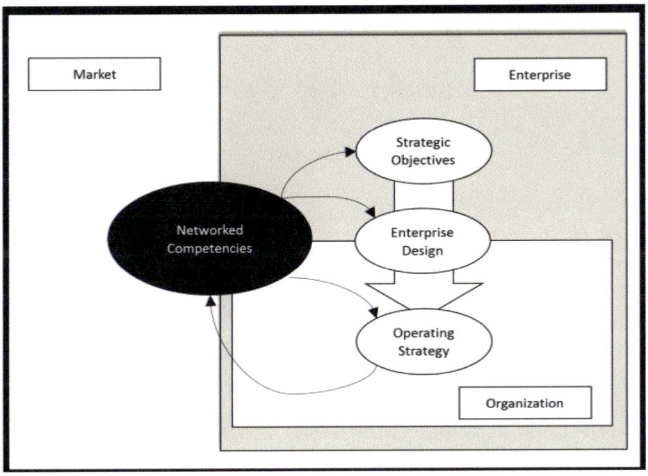

Networked Competencies bundle capabilities relevant to deliver a product or service to the end-consumer based on innovation focus and outcomes.

This chapter unpacks that statement by walking step-by-step through the Networked Competencies approach in looking at industry verticals and value networks, setting us up for when we speak to enterprise and organization-specific view of strategic objectives and competitive considerations.

***

Industry Use-Cases

I will use four industry use-cases through the balance of this book. While imperfect and stereotypical, they enable a level of specificity.

- Retailer. Think Walmart or Primark - fundamentally about selling products to consumers: omni-channel presence (meaning brick & mortar locations, e-commerce and mobile commerce capable); some quantity of private label design; distribution management capabilities (meaning managing the supply chain potentially from manufacture through to consumer - and reverse - but not necessarily owning all those assets); some distribution centers owned.
- Healthcare Products Provider. Think Johnson & Johnson or Pfizer: multi-national; significant research & development and product development for medical devices and pharmaceuticals (including requisite regulatory processes); manufactures a

portion of their product - outsources balance to third parties; distribution management capabilities; marketing sales channels to medical practices and retailers; mix of standard product - some very customized to a specific practitioner or consumer.

- IT Software & Services Vendor. Think Microsoft or IBM: R&D and application / product development; internal services to help potential customers to develop business cases, conduct readiness assessments, project management, systems integration, implementation, and post-implementation support; offers application hosting in the cloud; marketing / sales channels to business segments and systems integration houses.
- Integrated Financial Institution. Think Bank of America or JP Morgan Chase: mega bank with strong footprints in retail, commercial, and investment banking; omni-channel - including a distribution of ATMs; private banking capabilities for high net worth individuals; offers consumer products such as credit

cards and mortgage origination; payments offerings (credit cards and Treasury services); potentially trading / investment components.

***

The core process for depicting the Networked Competencies for a given sector takes the following steps (details will follow below):

1. Start from the point of view of the customer and market
2. Identify activities and outcomes within the customer and market, considering multiple channels and contexts for the transactions and extend the time frame with activities leading up to the transaction and after.
3. Identify the capabilities needed to support these activities.
4. Group these capabilities based upon as-is innovation focus and outcomes.
5. Place your organization's value network, competition, and best-in-class (could be outside your industry) into the networked competencies.
6. Assess the relative performance of key players and value of each competency.

Sticky Notes and a large white board are the best medium (that or the holographic visualization tools used by Tony Stark in the Avengers and Iron Man movies — when such is available to the market) for this exercise as they support the iterations of idea generation and categorization (through colors and placement).

Note: I will use a hypothetical Smart Apparel manufacturer to illustrate sample outcomes of the Networked Competencies sequence given relative simplicity compared to the industry use cases above.

1. Start from point of view of the customer and market

The starting point for networked competencies is the end-consumer within your market (e.g., Walmart shopper or mid-sized business seeking a loan). Your point of view pivots later in this process but start, grounded and firmly rooted, from the end-consumer's perspective.

The end-consumer may not be your enterprise's direct customer. If you provide supply chain services to our use-case Retailer or Healthcare Products Provider, start with the end-consumer. If you provide business services to multiple verticals, start with a specific sector. Specificity helps.

Or you may have multiple consumers or markets to consider. In the case of our Integrated Financial Institution, there will be both retail and corporate customers and different transaction types. The Healthcare Products Provider use case gets even more complex, factoring in end consumers but also government, insurance companies, and businesses. But the end customer remains the patient.

Understand the existential significance of the end-consumer, customer and market selection: without overdoing it, they are the purpose and backbone for which you are investing your valuable time and attention.

In the case of the Smart Apparel manufacturer, the end-consumer is straight-forward (ie., the individual wearing the garment) and the 'smart' associated with registering biometric or kinetic data.

2. Identify activities and outcomes within that scope

The goal of this step is to document the scope 'market' more specifically – defined by the related activities and outcomes.

To start, define and begin at the 'moment of truth' transaction from the end-consumer point of view (buying a shirt, selecting a software vendor, selecting a benefits program). Note there could also be several moments of truth: for example, retail payments have several key interaction points including whether or not the individual chooses to have that card, whether or not they use the card for a given transaction, and when they pay-off the card balance (if relevant). But, define your transactions and identify the relevant activities.

Then work backwards to pre-transaction activities that led to the transaction (e.g., research, brand exposure and interaction, assessing best healthcare plan based upon historical uses and comparisons with similar population, supply chain from manufacture to potentially kit[6] & convey product to delivery points).

Then go forward and consider post-transaction activities (e.g., return product, support / maintain, train / educate, ensure compliance with prescription, enhance product).

---

[6] By 'kit' I mean combining product components from multiple origins which could mean everything from throwing a power cord in with a TV, upgrading PC firmware prior to distribution, assembling parts for a baby stroller to ship to distributors or assembling knee replacement kit to ship to a surgeon.

Referring to our Retailer use-case, follow the supply chain backwards and forwards, (potential) activities include designing the product, selecting a supplier, manufacturing / transporting / storing, retailers selecting and ordering the product, transporting the product into the retailer's supply chain, executing payment (between all of the parties), delivering the product, managing the return, and managing inventory at end of lifecycle.

Also consider multiple contexts and channels (and interaction) in the three time frames (transaction, pre- and post-), for example:

- Brand exposure might take place in a magazine (read on an iPad or hard copy) or television or research through searches, social media links, and web-boards — or touching / feeling at a physical location.
- Purchase and pick-up may be done at a physical outlet or may be separated — purchase via smart phone for pick-up at a hub (train station locker, UPS store or gas station).
- Feedback regarding efficacy may be requested of the consumer or directly obtained from the device itself.

The use-case Healthcare Products Provider may be similar but significantly more regulatory tracking complexities involved (including approvals) and degrees of customization to medical practitioners / consumers.

Once applied to the end-consumer point of view consider the related activities from potential intermediaries' point of view. A provider of supply chain services to our use-case Retailer should be looking at activities and outcomes from both end-consumer and customer (Retailer) points of view.

Iterate a few times. Don't self-edit too much. Capture 'notes to self' in a different color (as I have in the Smart Apparel example). Purposely divert attention to another subject for a reset and come back to identify a potential miss. Consider where you are in sharp focus versus more fuzzy, but, otherwise move on.

Sample Activities and Outcomes (Step 2) for Smart Apparel Manufacturer.

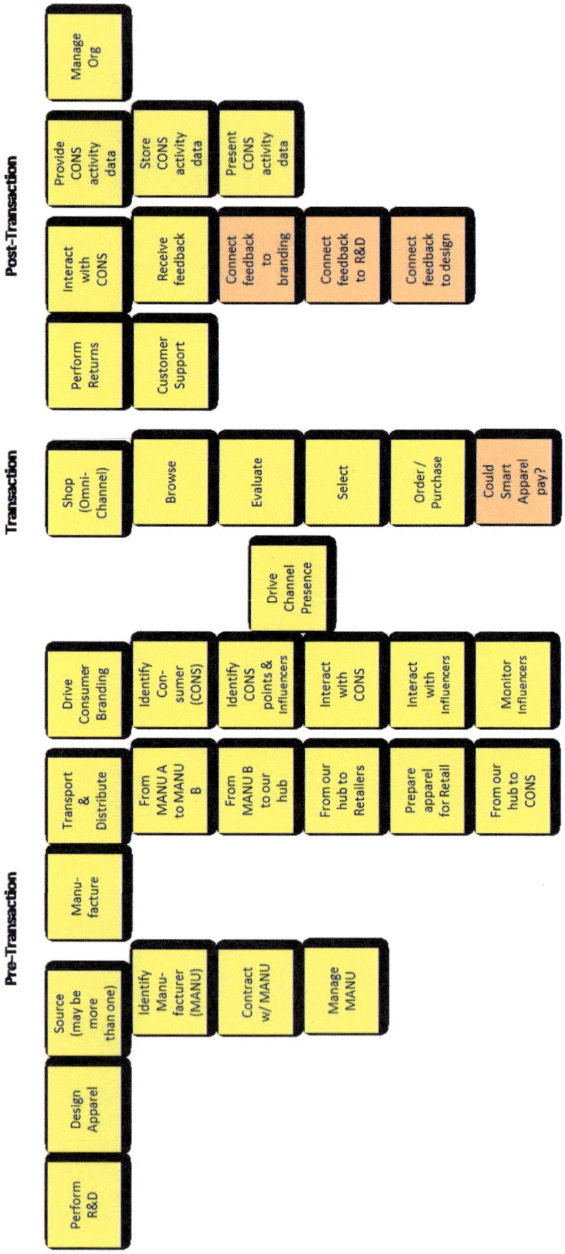

***

Acknowledge Type 1 & Type 2 Thinking

In his 2011 "Thinking Fast and Slow", Nobel Memorial Prize in Economics winner Daniel Kahneman distinguishes between two types of thinking: fast, instinctive, emotional (Type 1); slower, more deliberative and logical (Type 2).

To address energy levels — allow the process to iterate. Take breaks. Be mindful that deliberated, Type 2, thinking is a consumable / finite resource.

To help an activity be specific, be clear about the outcome and/or any decisions involved. Start each item with a verb.

***

3. Identify the capabilities needed to support those activities

With the activities captured, place straw model capability categories as 'swim-lanes' as depicted below to populate capabilities. The purpose of the straw model capability categories is to spur thinking and coverage. Generic categories — subject to change given granularity and relevance — include:

- Information — what data is necessary - and what needs to be done with it - to perform an activity; what data emerges from the activity
- Physical — meaning 'real world' assets
- Logistics — movement (and coordination) of products and people over time
- Experience — product and service design
- Technology
- Services — value to be provided by the applied resources
- Transaction Accounting — tracking / executing movement of funds, ownership (arguably a subset of Information) but is double sided — someone pays / someone is paid
- Risk — identifying, managing, mitigating
- Regulatory

During this process, capture (verb first, adequately specific and concrete) capabilities and assets necessary to support each of the activities in the prior step.

You may find that certain capabilities and assets ‘cross’ multiple lanes or activity steps — and that is absolutely fine and expected. The objective is to capture the set of capabilities.

You may also find that information, in particular, ties to capabilities and activities elsewhere on the process. In the example of the Smart Apparel Manufacturer below, properly evaluating bids coming from potential source points may require knowing transportation and distribution costs from the origins (more part of the supply chain process) so I’ve captured them in an alternate color.

Identifying Capabilities (Step 3) for Smart Apparel Manufacturer within the

Sourcing function

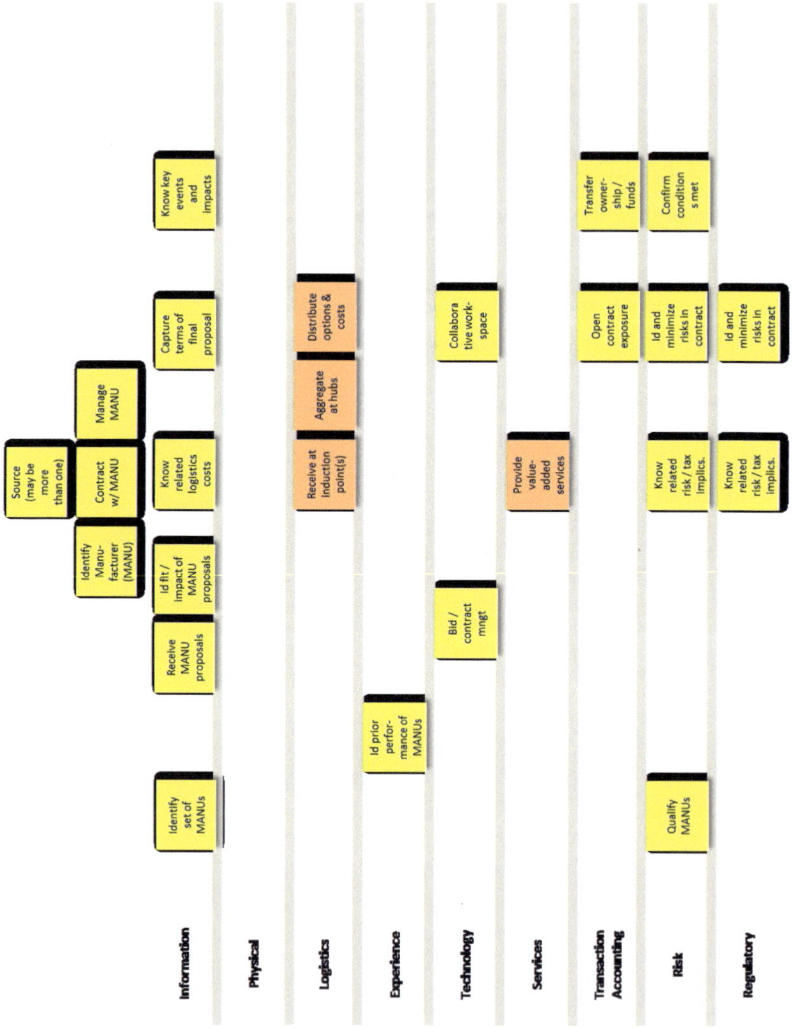

Plan to repeat this a few times to ensure you cover data for outlying areas in adequate detail — there will be a natural and understandable comfort to dwell on, and further detail, activities closer to home market.

Again, avoid editing too much, but take note perspectives on importance (e.g., a need to have or nice to have, importance to the customer[7]) and trends (e.g., emerging differentiator).

4. Bundle those capabilities based upon as-is innovation focus and outcomes

The goal of this step is to obtain our value networks' set of competencies.

Review each capability and ensure you understand the outcome or value-add provided by same — then characterize it by 'as is' Innovation Focus and Outcome.

Let's unpack that by looking at how Innovation Focus plus Outcome yield Networked Competencies — taking each step at a time.

Innovation Focus ...

---

[7] Delivering more service capability than a customer needs- or is willing to pay for – is either an intentional investment or waste.

If you have a dollar, where would you invest it? When key tactical decisions are made in the light of uncertainty (e.g., whether to move forward with product launch, whether to acquire safety stock) what rules of thumb should be applied?

An organization establishes its business model[8] as a particular mix of product, service, and price delivered via a specific method (product interface, user experience, internal processes, etc.). Innovation focus is about the trajectory taken *from that point* — about building an operational strategy and processes that create acceleration for change.

Innovation focus is baked into organizations — specifically the processes and culture hard-wired into the organization that drive not only experimentation and development but also operational decisions and surrounding tacticals.

The original catalyst for innovation focus came from John Hagel III and Marc Singer's "Net Worth" (almost as an apparent afterthought in the book, but highlighted within "Unbundling the Corporation" in a McKinsey Quarterly article in 2000 Number 3). I include the key summary table — as published — herein.

---

[8] Using 'business model' as a summarized depiction of the business characterizing the value the business creates to the customer, the organizational platform, the financial flows (capitalization, costs and revenues) and how it relates to industry networks.

Rethinking the Traditional Organization

	Customer Relationship	Product Innovation	Infrastructure
Economics	High cost of customer acquisition makes it imperative to gain large wallet share; economies of scope are key	Early market entry allows for a premium price and large market share; speed is the key	High fixed costs make large volumes essential to achieve low unit costs; economies of scale are the key
Competition	Battle for scope; rapid consolidation; a few big players dominate	Battle for talent; low barriers to entry; many small players thrive	Battle for scale; rapid consolidation; a few big players dominate
Culture	Highly service oriented; customer comes first mentality	Employee centered; coddling the creative stars	Cost focused; stress standardization; predictability and efficiency

A different angle on this conversation emerged from Harvard Business School professor (and general management guru on all things disruption and innovation) Professor Clayton Christiansen's resources-processes-values (RPV) theory: "that resources (what a firm has), processes (how a firm does its work) and values (what a firm wants to do) collectively define an organization's strengths as well as its weaknesses and blind spots." While this theory was grounded in disruption — and more specifically why good operating established companies struggle with adjusting to disruptive forces — this also applies to innovation focus: organizations, given their specific resources-processes-values, (a) will be inherently more capable at some things than others and (b) more capable to develop along certain lines over time.

The notion that an organization should have a specific innovation focus may create some unease as there may be a perspective that enterprises need to do all things well and concerns whether setting bounds limit the organization.

Regarding the concern that enterprises need to do all things well: organizations, of course, need to be mindful of all their dimensions (quality, customer satisfaction, cost per unit, etc.). But, realistically, innovation is needed to be competitive and choices / priorities made. The priorities should be made evident throughout the organization through resource investments, practiced processes, demonstrated culture and choices of innovation — and particularly in the eyes of front-line decision-makers.

Regarding the latter concern (i.e., whether setting bounds limits the organization): theoretically an organization built to build and operate communications networks could reinvent itself as a consumer solutions play but pragmatically, overcoming organizational behavioral momentum is hard as there is still the core business driving key decisions (e.g., capital investments) and an entrenched culture that will not change without heavy investment and time. Acknowledging predispositions and gauging the strategy's fit with current resources, processes, culture and innovation focus may actually spur more creative thinking by introducing constraints —and yield a more successful outcome.

Enterprises, however, may have multiple innovation focus areas. Our use-case Healthcare Products Provider starts with a customer focused sales group, product focused R&D and a process / scale focused group with manufacturing and supply chain management. There is potential value to loosely joining these organizations in the portfolio-firm operating strategy we'll discuss further in Part III — but linking them too tightly potentially constrains their individual value and ability to accelerate.

Each capability should be characterized therefore as scale, product or customer oriented.

… Plus Outcome …

Not every capability within the same Innovation Focus is part of the same competency. The scale-based manufacturing capability of the use-case Healthcare Products Provider is distinctly different to the supply chain / distribution management. (Although — regulatory aspects aside — there is a good deal of overlap between the supply chain / distribution management skill sets across our Retailer). The resources and processes invested in as part of the manufacturing capability won't directly contribute to the supply chain / distribution capability.

So adding Outcome as a criterion helps to further narrow the trajectory and clarify the competency in question.

… Yield Networked Competencies

Getting much more specific here is difficult (below is the set of networked competencies — including description and innovation focus — for our Smart Apparel manufacturer) but a few sign-posts may help:

- You should have a set of competencies with a mix of scale / cost, product and customer focus. The exact number isn't specific, but will reflect a degree of relevant granularity.
- You should see different scales across the competencies. There are vast differences in scale between an organization with a designers' eye on eyewear vs one that most effectively transports that product from origin to destination vs a media curator who brings together lifestyle points of a customer segment vs a lens manufacturer.

- Understand who is packaging the competencies into a product or service and, possibly, who is curating or selecting the product, service or content for the consumer.
- You should have a sense of emerging competencies versus more mature / standard / ticket to play.
- Most importantly, you should have a few question marks — situations where you have current companies or markets that seemingly span into several competencies. For now, note it. We'll come to this shortly.

Bundling Capabilities into Competencies (Step 4) for Smart Apparel Manufacturer. Note — I have described the competencies here both by outcome as well as focus area (Customer relationship, Product Innovation, or Infrastructure).

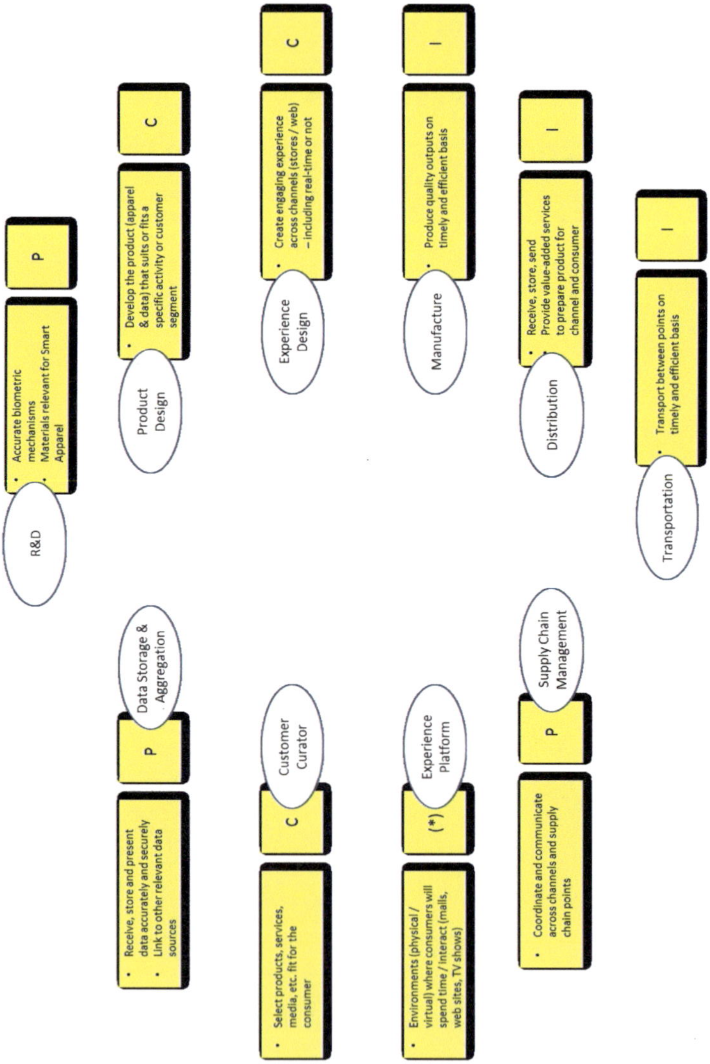

5. Place your organization's value network, competition, and best-in-class into the networked competencies.

With your networked competencies plotted, note the players in three categories:

- Ring One (Enterprise and Partners) — your organization and partners involved in providing or delivering competencies that are part of your offering
- Ring Two (Competitors) — same for your competitors
- Ring Three (Best Practices) — other organizations you see as best practice representatives

Graphically you could represent as concentric circles, again using Sticky Notes, but odds are this should be relatively quick as you have been working through this process and likely comparing to real world.

Note you may find odd juxtapositioning across the rings where a partner / supplier in ring one could also be a competitor — such as the Apple / Samsung relationship, where the companies compete intensively in the smart phone space although Samsung is a key supplier of chips for Apple's iPhone and displays for other Apple products.

Uncomfortable perhaps, but accurate.

Also discomforting? Almost everyone else in rings one, two, and even three is a potential competitor (this subject will be explored further in Part II). Or partner of course.

Relationships are complicated.

6. Assess the relative performance of key players and value of each competency

There are several assessment approaches you can take, depending upon your intended level of analytical rigor ranging from qualitative from an internal point-of-view and keeping it anecdotal through to detailed quantified analysis.

At least four points-of-view should be considered to some degree:

- ***Benchmark* from Customer point of view** — It's a short hop from capabilities, competencies, and rings into a questionnaire or session with customers to understand how they look at things, what they value and how they gauge performance (e.g., key differentiators, relative performance of competitors).

- **Understand the Customer's *attention field* as it relates to this space** — What are they knowledgeable about? What do they *want* to be knowledgeable about? Where do they spend time? Where do they *want* to spend time (or where do they *not want* to spend time)? Where *should* they spend their time?
- **Assess *economic value*** — If the customer spends $100 on a good or service, how does that distribute out across the competencies?
- **Map *information flow*** — Start from the end customer point of view at the points of transaction and identify the as-is information inputs (leading to a decision / action) and outputs. What information gets captured – or should be captured - and by whom?

Choosing the right level of detail is important: conducting highly researched quantitative analysis on how economic value distributes across a value network could take significant time and resource whereas an internal held Q&A session might fall short. Look for a range of perspectives and gauge the needed analysis based on impact.

Close

The Networked Competencies approach looks at the market landscape and activities from an organizational capability - and innovation focus - point-of-view.

While on the surface, it may come across as 'process-y' and theoretical, the networked competencies lens grounds *Deliberate Performance*, considering how specialization and focus alters the market landscape, eventually connecting with how decisions are both distributed and aligned in the organization, and how resources-processes-culture-innovation focus are developed.

Operating Strategy and Tacticals will circle us back into developing competencies. But from here we begin move into the point where networked competencies and aligning decisioning overlap - Strategic Objectives.

But first a brief digression into the pragmatic value of purpose.

Digression — Pragmatic Value of Purpose

'Purpose' plays a very significant role in organizational performance and comes up several times throughout this book. Too often, purpose in management literature is framed as a trade-off between 'doing good' and the bottom-line – thereby neglecting the direct importance of purpose on bottom-line results. In the context of this book, purpose plays four key roles: branding, creating organizational drive, enhancing performance through associate engagement, and supporting decision-making.

Branding

There's a *branding* aspect where world-bettering purpose can differentiate a company in the eyes of consumers — think TOMS, starting with 'One for One' — matching every pair of shoes purchased with a new pair for a child in need — and extending into eyewear and coffee (and clean water).

Similar models have been implemented by Warby Parker (eyewear), Smile Squared (toothbrushes) and One World Futbol (soccer balls).

Other examples might include Johnson & Johnson as communicated by the start of the credo ("We believe our first responsibility is to the doctors, nurses, and patients, to mothers and fathers and all others who use our products and services....") or Chipotle's focus on 'Food with Integrity.'

Creating Organizational Drive

Second, purpose creates *organizational drive*, acting as the equivalent of an individual's limbic system, thereby helping organizations to make decisions and avoid analysis-paralysis.

Some quick background: as individuals, we are generally counseled that we make best decisions based on logic. Research from Professor Antonio Damasio, Professor of Neuroscience at the University of Southern California, fundamentally changed that view, highlighting the function of emotion in effective judgment and decision-making in his oft-cited 1994 "Descartes' Error":

> Building on the work of many thinkers in the field, including Marsel Mesulam, Lennart Heimer, and Mortimer Mishkin, Damasio showed that patients with damage to the part of the prefrontal cortex that

> processes emotions (or, in a way, "listens" to them) often struggle with making even routine decisions.
>
> A patient named Elliot was among the first to raise this weird possibility in Damasio's mind 20 years earlier. Elliot had been an exemplary husband, father, and businessman. But he began to suffer from severe headaches and lose track of work responsibilities. Soon, his doctors discovered an orange-sized brain tumor that was pushing into his frontal lobes, and they carefully removed it, along with some damaged brain tissue. It was during his recovery that family and friends discovered (as Damasio put it) that "Elliot was no longer Elliot." Though his language and intelligence were fully intact, at work he became distractible and couldn't manage his schedule. Faced with an organizational task, he'd deliberate for an entire afternoon about how to approach the problem. Should he organize the papers he was working on by date? The size of the document? Relevance to the case? In effect, he was doing the organizational task too well, considering every possible option—but at the expense of achieving the larger goal. He could no longer effectively reach decisions, particularly personal and social ones, and despite being repeatedly shown this flaw, he could not correct it.[9]

The limbic system, within an individual, facilitates decision making through a mechanism that appears to speed or enhance rational judgment.

Jumping back up to the organization level, engrained purpose performs a similar function — creating the drive to convert analytical assessments into actioned decisions. Without purpose, one runs a heavy risk of analysis-paralysis.

Enhancing Performance through Associate Engagement

---

[9] Harvard Business Review, January 2006. "Decisions and Desire"

Third, purpose enhances performance through associate *engagement* — knowing and believing in why the work is important positively contributes to individual and organizational performance. I will have more to say about this several times throughout the book.

Supporting Decision-Making

Finally, a clear and shared purpose supports *decision-making* - both in aligning team members to common objectives and creating heuristics — or rules of thumb — and to facilitate making decisions. Faced with a moment of truth, does the associate balance the needs of the customer, prioritize his or her employment by sticking to process, or perform the assigned task?

To repeat the point — I am not advocating that every enterprise or organization has a social mission. The purpose can be more competence-based ("To make the best engineered widgets") but stating and demonstrating purpose is extraordinarily valuable for all the reasons mentioned above.

PART II - STRATEGIC OBJECTIVES

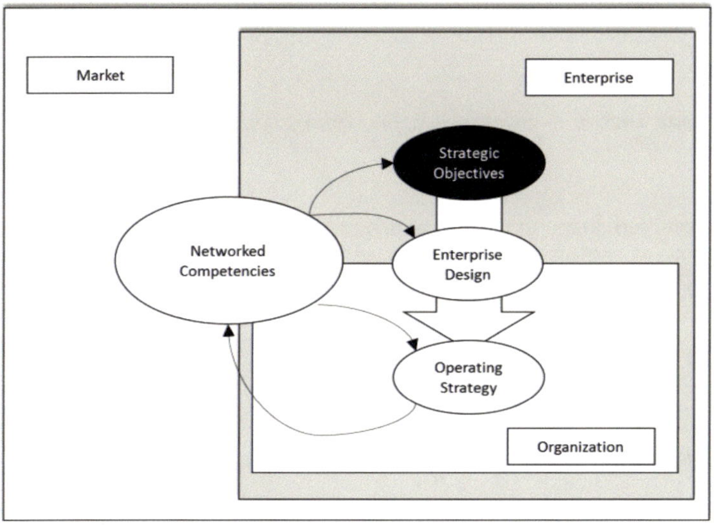

Strategic objectives are selections made by management in context of market developments and internal resources, processes, culture and innovation focus (RPCI) that set the foundation for decisioning — setting goals, approaching and measuring those goals and agreeing *not* to do certain things.

In Part II, I'll begin with tactics used to create distinctive value propositions ('yang tactics'), tactics used to solidify the organization's own position ('yin tactics') and then pull it together to talk strategic process and outcomes. (Note — I am using yin-yang here both in a more traditional sense: yang as a harder and aggressive, yin as more pliable and supple — as well as the 'two sides of the same coin' view as both, for example, consider value proposition.)

Yang Tactics — Integration, Modularization, Next Gen, Subversion

Having walked through the Networked Competencies approach in Part I, you should have a good foundation of the *as-is* external market environment and how the enterprise / organization fits into it.

The initial question then is: how should the enterprise orient its value proposition and business model for greatest likelihood of success?

There is always the choice to replicate a product or service and compete, head-to-head, on brand, experience, features and price. And while that's a time-honored strategy ("if equally matched, we can offer battle" [10]) the key opportunity entrants should seek is to out-flank ("Hence to fight and conquer in

[10] Sun Tzu, The Art of War

all your battles is not supreme excellence; supreme excellence consists in breaking the enemy's resistance without fighting." [11]) — leveraging key networked competencies and knowledge already in place within the enterprise.

This out-flanking lesson is also highlighted in early research on disruption:

> Empirical findings showed that incumbents outperformed entrants in a sustaining innovation but underperformed in a disruptive innovation context... Incumbents (sensibly) listen to their existing customers and concentrate on sustaining innovations as a result... Incumbents' focus on their existing customers becomes institutionalized in internal processes that make it difficult for even senior managers to shift investment to disruptive innovations.[12]

Which brings us to four yang tactics to be discussed here in further depth — modularization, integration, next gen, and subversion.

Modularization

As previously stated, a low transaction cost environment drives specialization and *modularization*. This is, in fact, core to Christiansen's Value Chain Evolution (VCE) theory:

> Industries tend to evolve from states of interdependence, where leading firms need to be vertically integrated, to modularity, in which

[11] Sun Tzu, The Art of War

[12] "The Big Idea: What is Disruptive Innovation? Clayton M Christensen, Michael Raynor, Rory McDonald December 2015 Harvard Business Review

> specialist firms that are responsible for critical pieces of the value chain and produce key product components can earn a disproportionate share of value in an industry.[13]

To make it more concrete, modularization is going to market with a specific and narrow value proposition that is already likely embedded in some other incumbent's value chain.

Google at its outset is a poster child for this: focusing initially on search — a very specific piece of functionality — and building from that 'humble' beginning. (I will return to its evolution to Alphabet in Part III).

Quintiles is another prime example: in-sourcing — and scaling up — clinical development for bio-pharmaceutical firms that, as of late 2015, had "more than 32,000 employees working in about 100 countries" and "helped develop or commercialize all of the top–100, best-selling drugs on the market in 2013."

Modularization centers on deep content knowledge and capability of the process or product in focus and, oftentimes, the customer won't be the end-consumer in question. So, in the case of Quintiles, their customer are the bio-pharmaceutical firms who previously housed that capability – not the end-consumer.

---

[13] "Seeing What's Next" Clayton M Christensen, 2004.

Integration

The opportunities to out-flank are not only in modularization.

Integration — or bundling distinctive products and services — can create value through improved product performance (e.g., OnStar or other onboard automotive navigation systems obviating needs for separate Garmin or TomTom devices) or through improved / streamlined customer experience — potentially targeted to a specific customer segment.

In the case of improved product performance, integration will more likely involve deep content knowledge and capability of the process or product in focus or otherwise will tend to be more structured around understanding of customers' needs and triggers.

The method of integration can range from embedded to available and the capability may be either contracted by the integrator or owned.

Amazon.com's path since the early days represented a relentless focus on the customer — both to be the one-stop shop for retail purchasing (consider both the expanse of product and focus on experience) but also the fulfillment /execution.

Apple completely re-built the user experience surrounding computing to make it more humane when they came up with the iPhone and iPad and the business models / processes involving apps to drive functionality.

Less broad examples of integration include:

- Publications such as The Week [http://www.TheWeek.com] — aggregating / curating content across a broad array of international media.
- Wells Fargo, among retail financial institutions, has pushed hard (legal filings mid 2015 suggest potentially too hard in some areas) to cross-sell core banking, lending, payment, investment, wealth management and insurance products.
- Etsy has created a multi-function marketplace for "the creative entrepreneurs who use Etsy to sell what they make or curate, the shoppers looking for things they can't find anywhere else, the manufacturers who partner with Etsy sellers to help them grow."

Next Gen

Next gen reflects same service at materially lower price due to declining differentiation and cost-cutting enabled by (a) alternate delivery models for similar services or cutting back wasteful / unneeded services and expenses and (b) certain features specific to information technology.

In the former case, a new entrant is by no means obligated to replicate the incumbent's structure or investment path. For example:

- An IT Software & Services entrant builds an industry specific data visualization application with built-in links to leading applications. If there is good adoption, it could become a leverage point to develop additional functionality and encroach on the incumbents' core applications, thereby becoming Next Gen.
- A Main Street retailer in a small town selects, orders, stocks / displays and returns — leveraging e-commerce retail platforms (e.g., Zappos, Nordstrom, Amazon) to accumulate and return inventory within 30 days in 'trunk' fashion.
- Take the more classic disruptive approach highlighted in Professor Christiansen's work, for example, providing a lower frills offering to a lower demand sub-segment of the market.

In the latter, technology specific fundamentals introduce specific changes as well, such as:

- Increased impact from innovation — epitomized by Moore's Law, but carried out along multiple paths. Changing lines of code or screen layout resulting in improved process or experience can be done much more fluidly (and multivariate evaluations more quantitatively tested) than doing so across hundreds of outlets and individual disconnected interactions.
- Leveraging individuals' cookie crumb trails (mobile devices now signaling physical trails as well as cookies capturing virtual trails) — along with incorporating multivariate evaluations to test hypotheses — create opportunities for tailoring and customizing.
- Over-turning 'classic' information asymmetries — from physics to economics, asymmetries create dynamics. High profile 'gig' economy plays like Airbnb, Uber, or Elance create value in soaking up underused assets. Moving information across the world at minimal marginal cost allows companies to source processes to lower wage regions of the world. Immediate reach across international boundaries coupled with national differences in healthcare pricing rules & regulations creates hosts of arbitrage opportunities. Consider how the 'Internet of Things' creates an information pool that can be leveraged in field of insurance / risk assessment to better provide risk related information to insurers

as it captures information on speed, location, acceleration, braking, pedal position, driving patterns, time of day, traffic, etc.[14]

- Incremental distribution costs and marginal expenses (within a similar scale) — so the potential for steep price declines and volatility is significant. This aspect should be of particular concern to technology or information companies who have built up significant overhead expenses (services divisions, facilities, acquisitions) and rolled them into pricing as it creates space for next gen competitors at the significantly lower price point.

Subversion

Whereas next gen is effectively a similar value proposition at significantly lower price point, subversion is about repositioning *clichéd* aspects of the sector to subvert — and break through — the customer's field of attention.

According to Wikipedia, subversion "refers to a process by which the values and principles of a system in place are contradicted or reversed." So if the expectation is that a laundromat is an unfortunate place to go, subvert that

---

[14] Initial types of information (e.g., gauging driving safety habits, gauging personal individual activity) have a straight forwardly positive effect on both sides; genetic predispositions create greater complexity.

expectation. If retail banking branches are staid and less than inspiring, how to get people to want to spend time there.

Yang Tactics & Networked Competencies

Looking at these through Networked Competencies' lens is helpful for several reasons:

1. The Networked Competencies approach — through activities and capabilities and then bundling — should open up questions about current and potential product bundles and what is accepted as normal industry practice. (Try asking "what is the minimum acceptable level of customer service we can provide"[15] and understand the relevant cost implications).
2. The approach also helps identifying potential *Lily Pad* (the visual of hopping to another competency underlying the name 'lily pad')[16] strategic opportunities – and guide discussions about pivoting[17], meaning that an enterprise or organization should pursue growth

[15] Credit to my colleague Graham Scott for being the first individual I heard to pose this question.
[16] Will return to describing and executing Lily Pad strategies in the Digression following Part III – Enterprise Design but, for now, note the execution points noted throughout this book apply.
[17] Pivoting typically used in the context of start-ups or entrants means iteratively changing the business model to better fit the customer need.

opportunities that leverage its competencies, its knowledge of the industry / customers, or its resources-processes-culture-innovation focus to identify potential markets.

3. Identifying high priced aspects of the competency rings that are also relatively mature could help identify relevant next gen targets either for market entry, initiative and partnership selection.
4. Highlights the opportunity within modularizing the back room, non-customer-differentiating tasks. Not suggesting everyone should pursue insourcing accounts receivable and cash application for example, but there are opportunities there as well to be considered — it's often not about the customer fronting activity.

Two final points:

The yang tactics are not mutually exclusive. If our reference Financial Institution sets up a revamped retail personal financial management hub — think mall-based Starbucks type environment with a Genius Bar with some low key Personal Financial Experts supported by a technical platform that has an aggregated view of your financial transactions and access to a suite of services — advisory, personal information protection, etc. — you have both integration and subversion. Though I would still track back to Competencies when thinking about how to execute.[18]

The language here can be tricky. 'Disruption' is often used to describe a significantly changed proposition of any sort although I am mindful that Professor Christiansen and his team have a very specific thing in mind when they refer to 'disruption.' I have opted therefore to talk about 'out-flanking' and various specific market approaches of doing so.

***

Perspective Taking

Direct input from customers or other credible individuals can be helpful to prime conversations requiring different perspectives.

In the specific strategy conversation, there is both an *Incumbent* perspective — meaning how could this be applied

[18] There's a wealth of source material out there regarding Design processes but it's typically about framing the problem, creating a new – human - perspective using constraints, priming, and/or outside individuals and vetting through opportunities.

to a current space — and an *Entrant* perspective — meaning how could this be applied in a new market, segment or sub-segment. Both must be considered.

Both starting points — incumbent and entrant — have relative competitive advantages and disadvantages: incumbents will know idiosyncratic details, possess tacit knowledge based on experience and will be known to the market —but prior experience, decisions (back to the resources-processes-culture-innovation focus discussions), and risk aversion can shackle thinking, and size and need to move the growth meter may cause incumbents to discount opportunities that entrants may otherwise exploit, pursue and grow.

Entrants benefit from being able to set the terms of how they approach the market — focusing on a specific sub-market through tailoring the product or exploiting lower cost delivery methods. Entrants can also benefit from *beginner's mind* and not presuming what they can or cannot do.

More broadly, it's important to consider all available perspectives with the objective of making the decision. Take the time to consider the questions from different points of view. Talk to customers. Talk to industry players. Talk to expert third parties. Weigh the outputs openly and pragmatically.

But then decide and capture key reasons for the decision. Odds are you'll have been wrong in parts — it's a complex environment after all — but if you've executed well against a reasonably accurate strategy, odds are that you're in a good position.

***

Yin Tacticals — Maintaining One's Position

Whereas yang tacticals focus on more of the attacking spirit and out-flanking competitors, yin tacticals emphasize pliability to protect current markets. So here we focus instead on critical importance of branding, reconnaissance, and creating / communicating white spaces.

Branding

Yang tactics discussed previously (e.g., integration, modularization, next gen, subversion) and segment targeting complicate the traditional competitive picture by adding the dimension of *how* the entrant chooses to compete. These alternate means of entry lessen the barriers to entry and, if successful, create platforms for entrants that can be leveraged for growth and movement upstream.

Reviewing some of the traditional barriers to entry from Porter's Five Forces:

Name	Description - Example	Applicability
Government & Regulatory	Formal or informal regulations and practices that legalize, prevent, induce or dis-incentive actions by governments, individuals or entities. Formal practices may include import tariffs, barring foreign participants or inducing entry through tax incentives, or regulatory language prescribing certain requirements (e.g., capital requirements for financial institutions).	Not straightforward. Conditions are specific to a country / market, time, and viewer. Different firms may view the rules as either an unscalable wall, a scalable wall preventing other competitors from getting in (and therefore greater profits), a scalable wall that can be further fortified after entry to reduce competitive field or simply uncertain but a risk worth taking given the opportunity.[19]

[19] The subject of government's role in the economy including *policy* areas (such as guiding education systems, setting out appropriate social safety nets such as

	Informal practices may include signaling favorable views towards consolidation.	
Patents & Intellectual Property (IP) Protection	A subset of Government & Regulatory but focusing on rules and regulations associated on IP internationally	Designed to protect intellectual property rights and create a barrier to entry. However, for the Incumbent, vigilance comes at a cost: implementing, monitoring and enforcing activity — particularly globally - is not cheap - and really only worth it for high stakes plays. While I am not advocating breaking IP laws, Entrants may factor likelihood and size of the legal risk and opt to enter. For those high stakes plays, however, the *threat* of IP battles can prevent Entrants from participation – thus chilling competition.[20]
Proprietary knowledge, asset specificity and investment	Up-front investment, either hard (machinery / capital) or soft (experience / knowledge) needed prior to entering a market that results in a cost advantage.	The fundamental assumption being the lower the investment, the greater likelihood of entry. If an Entrant applies a competency or specific knowledge to enter a market - and the

retraining for disrupted locales and roles) and *structural-dynamics* considerations (such as term limits on representatives and regulations, interactions of government and business, and how citizens should engage politics and legislation) is a crucial one at the current time and is out of scope of this book (and, frankly, merits its own).

[20] Governments are challenged with a difficult balancing act, encouraging innovation, investment, and competition. Again, a subject for another time.

		Entrant chooses how to compete - they could weaken the barrier considerably.
Economies of scale	Cost advantages obtained by greater size and scope — could be both direct (e.g.,fixed cost base over a large, established base of transactions) or indirect (e.g., leveraged in negotiating with vendors or governments)	*Economies of scale* figure prominently in traditional strategy as a barrier to entry in process / scale-driven businesses and enterprises. Once again though, how an entrant approaches (outlined in *Next Gen* previously) can circumvent aspects of the scale issue: addressing an underserved specific niche; applying an innovative business model or technology; etc.
Product differentiation, innovation and brand loyalty	How well established is the brand in the markets and the customers?	Product differentiation, innovation and brand loyalty remains the most significant and persistent barrier to entry and why it is so critical for incumbents to continue to innovate, nurture and distinguish their respective brands - to preserve and enhance their place on their customer's attention field. Certainly an entrant can try to elbow their way in via a distinctive value proposition but limitations of the customers' attention field provide incumbents the higher ground to start.

Customer's switching costs	Changing providers can cost customers — financially, time & attention to implement the change and behaviorally adjusting to the new processes. .	Customers' switching costs can impede a shift to Entrants, but, (a) if a distinctive value proposition is provided by the Entrant, switching costs may create only a temporary stay (potentially allowing time for the Incumbent to catch-up or jump over) (b) Entrant can specifically target the switching aspect in their value proposition (e.g., "We will pay termination fees") and (c) be mindful that, in certain areas, technology can be used to significantly cut down on switching costs as well (e.g., AWS Export / Import Snowball announcement).

For the Incumbent, there is pragmatically little to do to prevent an Entrant from entering in some form if the Entrant is intent on doing so. And counting on many of the traditional barriers to entry would be a mistake for the reasons noted above.

The Incumbent, therefore, should really have four concerns:

- Consider the benefits case and feasibility of influencing regulatory aspects.

- Dominate its place on the end-customer's attention field through brand strategy and innovation.
- Understand scalability of the Entrant's entry mechanism.
- Consider a potential defense by establishing a separate operating unit per Portfolio Enterprise that will be set-up in Part III.

The importance of branding is nothing new but its nature has expanded a bit. As an example, Havas Worldwide's Brand Relevance study (2013) drew from a survey of 10219 men and women in 31 countries and concluded both brand *trust* and *dynamism* were necessary to drive brand momentum:

- Trust reflected more traditional attributes— inherent quality of the brand's products and services; openness in brand communications; a brand's heritage and links to the past; and, for larger brands, the ability to combine global power and reach with local sensitivity and involvement ('multi-local' in Havas Worldwide's language).
- Dynamism is more where the change is taking place— both about purpose[21] beyond profits and interactivity across online and offline outlets — not just functionality but also interaction (and, I would

[21] There's that word again – but in this tying more to the social / stakeholder purpose.

highlight, experience and dopamine-triggers resulting from the interactions).

Purpose and interaction are not simply additional means to engage and lock in customers' headspace, but a critical aspect of yin tactics.

Reconnaissance

Outside of the context of companies' IT systems being hacked, reconnaissance or intelligence isn't discussed much today in the corporate world. Which is a shame.

Understanding direct competitors' organizations deeply based on demonstrated resource-processes-culture-innovation focus — and (selectively) listening to optics — provides a leg-up understanding strengths and weaknesses, areas of attention, and blind spots.

For example, companies on significant growth trajectories may be vulnerable due to diluted focus, creating a competitive opportunity (or concern if the scenarios apply to you), for example:

Scenario 1. The original purpose and flow that fueled the organization is 'professionalized' and parsed out into departments to deal with complexity and growth. Rational influx - getting more heads and experience around solving problems — is generally a good thing, but cultural influx and the new interests created, however, can chip away at the focus. The new Head of Sales, based on his or her past experience, may frame the economic requirements (base pay plus commission) required resulting in a sales team who "tick the boxes" but don't *get* the product.

Scenario 2. Product maturity, or demands, may create a new set of needs. The developers who put together a next gen warehouse management system may need to create a capability to support bringing to market (services such as benefits case development, implementation & integration project management) — to what extent do they develop the capability internally or rely on third parties?

Scenario 3. Growth brings its own challenges, particularly as firms scale. The customers and kinds of deals that fueled the initial growth are not the same to maintain the earlier growth rates, creating confusion in sales targeting and potentially a mismatch with current operational processes. Moving the dial to achieve steady growth for a start-up or mid-sized company is very different than doing so for a top tier firm regardless of sector.

These are simply example narratives, but understanding your competitors from a resources-processes-culture-innovation focus perspective is enlightening.

So for known direct competitors in Ring Two — and Entrants — know, learn from, leverage and adjust to their behaviors.

Competitive White Spaces & Econ-systems

Incumbents should consider — assuming they can — how they can actively shape perceptions to make their particular market arena less attractive — and another one more so to competitors.

In the former instance, Incumbents could prime market opportunities for market niches or adjacent or complementary services outside their competency area:

- IT Software & Services firms may opt for a product-centric approach internally and may therefore encourage the growth of a third party industry to support implementations.
- Could a large scale / cost leading retailer like Wal-mart, create an opportunity to 'wholesale' their supply chain expertise out to local small businesses?

Athenahealth's More Disruption Please (MDP) accelerator program — represents one approach. In Athenahealth's MDP's case, start-ups within the program receive funding, free office space, access to Athenahealth's platform of doctor customers for guidance, and legal input regarding regulatory / compliance. In return, they are built leveraging Athenahealth's clinical platform — and therefore increase the value of the platform.

Several benefits to consider here:

- Less direct competition in the Incumbent's current sphere
- Dependents create additional revenue and volume streams for the Incumbent's business
- Creation of a symbiotic ecosystem
- A portfolio of outlets — through the Dependents — ought to systemically reduce risk while Incumbent focuses on its core business(es).

Decisions — Process and Outcomes

The outcome of the Strategic Objectives process is to achieve the following:

- Identify and prioritize opportunities and threats
- Identify and prioritize areas to focus and invest into and those to stop or potentially divest or exit from

- Identify constraints, risks and assumed dependencies
- Identify and prioritize targets, commitments, reconnaissance activities and optics

Deselection

Strategic Objectives are as much about choosing what *not to do* as they are choosing what *to do* — particularly given today's scarcity of attention and stretched management bandwidth.

From a Networked Competencies point of view:

- If an enterprise has key competencies that don't align with one another, assess the relative performance and value of each and develop associated strategies (see Part III on Enterprise Design).
- If an enterprise has functions outside the competencies — and unrelated to key Operating Strategy tacticals (see Part IV) — strongly consider outsourcing.

From the perspective of setting aligned decisions / heuristics, the deliberate decision to stop doing something or de-prioritizing sends an important message about identity and focus — particularly in a climate when it's easy to simply say 'Yes' (and the challenge of executing is held for later).

Close

Going back to method, Networked Competencies inform and ground the Strategic Objectives process: inform in the sense that it helps to make sense of the market landscape and dynamics; ground in the sense that Who We Are and What We Do Well is based on explicit and implicit decisions in our organization's DNA (resources-processes-culture-innovation focus).

The yin-yang approach described reflects the interactive and dual natures of the strategic process and decisions.

A defined set of Strategic Objectives are the first critical decisions in the cycle that inform Enterprise Design and then Operating Strategy. We'll head there after a brief digression.

Digression - IT Vendor Partnerships

Looking more closely at IT vendor partnerships provides both a different look into networked competencies and some of the strategic elements discussed herein.

In brief, executing the standard IT due diligence checklist is important to review features, functions and pragmatics. But several additional elements are critical *in the early stages of evaluation*.

Know Your Business Case — Absolute vs Relative Value

Information Technology creates enormous *absolute* value by storing, conveying or transforming data in some form. (Likewise, not having a particular IT capability can become a substantial competitive disadvantage.)

But, once replicated across the competitive landscape (and efficiencies absorb inflationary pressures such as wage increases to hold pricing and competitors replicate your solution), the particular IT capability is no longer a differentiator and may yield, in the mid-term no *relative* value — *aside potentially from the perception that you introduced it.*[22]

From a market point of view — understand to what degree first mover advantage aligns with — and therefore underscores — your brand, value proposition or strategic focus. From an internal process point of view (will cover this more in Part IV), how does this enable your associates to focus less on performing tasks and more on profit-making decisions? Otherwise waiting on the market for the specific technology to mature (or tilting the market if you have the resources), next gen providers — and the inevitable price drop — may be a better choice.

From an internal point of view, understand the real impact on your business' operating and cost models and how that affects processes and decisions. Usually IT creates greater cost at the front end (set-up and configuration, emphasis on data-process quality) leading to benefits through improved operational scalability and more data about where we are (which leads to the importance of

---

[22] The differentiation of absolute v relative value is, by the way, an interesting one to consider in the context of valuations and, I think, has caused a great deal of confusion not only in valuations but broader economic metrics of productivity. But that's a deeper discussion for another time.

tools that better extract and present meaningful data with which to make decisions).

Note also the human factor: associates who performed tasks well may not easily transition to decision orientation.

Know the Product's Market Maturity

As a specific product / market develops, there is a familiar pattern of introducing new features and, as features are adopted, increasingly incorporating what were once differentiating features into base platforms.

IT products — particularly under a software-as-a-service (SAAS) model or as processing capabilities move into the cloud - speed up the innovation-to-mass adoption rate significantly as introducing new features can be as simple as adding a few lines of code.

Maturity is not a simple binary state and the pace of significant innovations may pause for a bit, but monitor the market in question for consolidation and slowing pace of substantive innovations is a way to gauge maturity — that should hint at consolidation and viable next gen providers on the horizon.

Know the Provider Resource-Process-Culture-Innovation Focus and Emergent Challenges

As a potential key partner — particularly if they play a key part towards achieving your strategic objectives — it is important to understand your IT provider from a resource-process-culture-innovation focus perspective. Some examples of how to approach:

- What's their story? Try to understand key decision points that affected their development — e.g., key customers around whom they developed their product; what metrics or dashboards do executives review daily.
- What is their core value compared to other providers? How would they say their product differentiates them? Can they point out legitimate cases where the competition might be a better place to go? What are the next two or three key areas of innovation?
- If on a significant growth path, how are they scaling (and introduce service / quality disciplines) while maintaining product focus. If a product takes off, there is challenging balance of product innovation, customer needs (and requisite support implementing and customizing), quality and scalability. How does the IT enterprise

support the services inevitably required to develop business cases, implementation / project management and integrations?

- Who are the stakeholders and what are their motives? Pursuit of - or maintenance of — unicorn valuations requires a viable growth narrative on the part of the IT provider. As a firm grows it gets harder to identify proportionate growth opportunities that move the dial - and smaller opportunities may not satisfy investment community nor attract necessary capital / management nurturing internally.
- With the burden of overhead, how to compete with next gen providers. Overhead more than likely is added as the sector matures, consolidation ensues, and the IT enterprise has potentially added a services group to its staffing. These costs — which for all the right reasons are then factored into pricing — create significant competitive opportunities for next gen providers.

Close

Again, the standard IT due diligence lists are important but I emphasized a few elements here for early consideration:

- Know your business case or why you are making the investment — both in the absolute and relative sense — and ensure you incorporate that throughout the process (selection, implementation and post-implementation review)

- Try to understand the maturity of the market for the particular product as that can impact timing and the kind of provider you are looking for
- Know the providers' RPCI and emergent challenges to gauge fit and understand potential risks

Direct takeaways aside, however, this digression also applies some of the subjects discussed thus far in the context of vendor / partner.

PART III - ENTERPRISE DESIGN

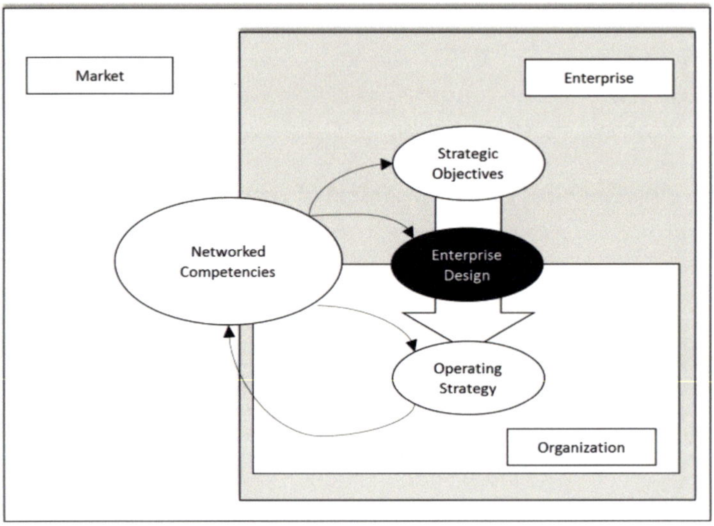

Strategic Objectives define the What, the Not-What (the "where to play") and, roughly, the How. The question then facing the Enterprise is how to set up the means to achieve the stated ends.

Maximizing operational performance in the organization is about selected focus as well as distributed and aligned decisions. Achieving that relies — among other things — on clarity and consistency across resources, processes, culture, innovation focus and targeted outcomes.

If your enterprise's Strategic Objectives line up with a clear, shared and aligned set of competencies, skim this chapter and the next important step becomes Operational Strategy (Part IV).

If not — and this applies for most, larger, companies — a different operating structure may be called for — referred to here as the *Portfolio Enterprise*.

Portfolio enterprises are not simply conglomerate holding companies or private equity holdings: rather there ought to be a strategy regarding how the portfolio of organizations creates value, structure the portfolio using *loosely joined principles* and execute accordingly. Others might point to the strategies and call them 'synergies' – to employ a greatly overused business term – but driving for more specificity here.

Strategic value of the portfolio

Portfolio enterprises create strategic value though either:

- Applying a key *capability* — and thereby a competitive advantage — to its constituent organizations, and/or

- Leveraging the *network* of organizations.

Where the capability approach emphasizes processes that add direct value to the constituent organizations, the network strategy emerges from the portfolio and is almost a by-product of the individual organizations' core value.

Applying Capability

'World class' complement. An enterprise may have a particularly strong competency — or set of competencies — to leverage value from acquisitions or different businesses, e.g.:

- A supply chain management capability handling garments could bolt-on a stable of lifestyle brands creating both scale to the firm and efficiency / effectiveness to the organization
- A content creative environment may bolt-on a stable of points-of-presence or channels to create an experience footprint
- A research and innovation lab may deliver the right resources, domain knowledge and cultural values to bolt-on ventures in similar space

Brand. An enterprise (e.g., Virgin) may have a strong brand following — driven by a combination of experience design, marketing, representation, and/or curating the right set of products — to create value by bringing the portfolio brand to a new product.

Management disciplines. An enterprise (e.g., Berkshire Hathaway) may have particularly low costs of capital, discipline in applying leading practice disciplines, etc., and bring those capabilities to create incremental value.

Leveraging the Network

Customer interaction information. In the highly publicized world of Big Data, leveraging customer touch point data is *passé* — but nevertheless relevant:

- Our use-case Integrated Financial Institution (now focusing on the retail arm) should use the customer data visible through payment and account transactions – and ideally through pre-transaction interactions - to create a fundamentally different relationship with its customers.
- The sales — relationship side of our Healthcare Product Provider test case is similar: use the information from interactions / knowledge gathering / relationship building in product design and supply chain components.

Mine transactions. Supply chains systems, payment processors, order systems, and search engines are all examples of systems at the center of massive quantities of data. Add to that the 'internet of things', acquiring data on the position and condition of assets and situation around those assets and things only multiply.

For example — consider potential implications of a consumer device that monitors your blood pressure / heart rate conditions based on family history, communicates with your insurance company, medical practice and potentially discounts based on good behavior.

Review the transactions and events resulting from customer interactions (direct person to person and through devices) and internal processes and consider how to potentially create value from that data.

Benefit from knowing and doing. Having a limited internal capability (e.g., performing a portion of your manufacturing or owning some of the transportation capability) provides real-world knowledge regarding a market sector, reducing the information asymmetries between you and your vendors, speaking the language, identifying potential pitfalls, and knowing lead / lag indicators — all of which will enable you to better empathize and negotiate with partners.

There is also a risk mitigation aspect here. If, for some reason a supplier goes awry, having the capability internally — whether to assist or supplant — creates value.

Risk. Hedging risk through a portfolio is a logical strategy: identifying key points of uncertainty (e.g., fuel prices, currency valuation) and participating in industries and roles that experience divergent outcomes from those changes (e.g., energy sector benefits from increased price of fuel, airlines are adversely impacted) is possible and may be attractive to some investors.

Tabling the question of whether we can practically *eliminate* risk through hedging, there is the question whether it's the enterprise's role to mitigate risk or whether it should be the investor or asset manager's role to do so. In my view, leadership should make the choice / argument and state their intent — and allow investors to decide whether to participate.

"Loosely Joined" Principles

The Enterprise is as strong as the weakest link

Pursuit of portfolio value is not an excuse to allow for sub-optimal performance of constituent organizations — and all the discussions regarding organizational performance discussed throughout this book remain in play.

And, in fact, there's risk that a wrong endeavour or acquisition — if it's not compatible, if the enterprise lacks the resources, if it fails to execute or innovate — could impact the whole enterprise.

Portfolio organizations should always be encouraged to work with best of breed partners: if that's internal, great; if it involves working with a third party, then they should (and communicate why).

Information needs to flow

Data should flow out of the organizations and generally be accessible enterprise-wide in granular, simple and transparent forms.

Portfolio enterprises add the requirement of information compatibility to other entities within the enterprise so integration, normalization or addition of attributes may all be required.

(Note — I return to the importance of information architecture, or IA, in Part IV but, bluntly speaking, I cannot easily see how a portfolio enterprise can be effective — and grow — without a strong IA.)

Default position should be as loose as possible

If the strategic value of the portfolio is based on leveraging a capability, there should be tight links between the portfolio enterprise parents and constituent organization's within the specific functions (e.g., if using a central supply chain team), brand / marketing teams, or, exclusively with management. Outside of that, they should maintain as much autonomy — and responsibility for their own success — as possible.

There will be arguments to centralize additional functions or decisions or push constituent organizations to partner with others in the portfolio (potentially through reward systems) — all for apparently logical reasons. Resist the urge though. Counter based on the long term, citing emphasis on driving self-reliance, excellence and innovation within the units.

For example, say our industry use case Integrated Financial Institution has an asset management unit — focused on several different investment / return profiles and a retail advisory unit. Should it obligate the retail advisory unit to work exclusively with the asset management unit? It could seem sensible at first glance (get more dollars into the asset management funds) but (a) that should naturally happen if the asset management unit performs well and (b) if it does not perform well, you are adversely impacting your retail advisory unit. So the short answer should be no.

Tactical considerations

Understand interaction of portfolio strategy and enterprise scalability and rate of growth

As noted previously a portfolio strategy based on network should benefit from growth (although the importance of maintaining the information architecture may impact rate of growth).

Those based on leveraging a specific capability — or capabilities — will likely see slower rate of growth due to increased integration requirements (processes, systems, culture) but scalability may also depend upon the nature of the capability leveraged:

- Process-based competencies (e.g., supply chain management) should scale well if there's good compatibility with new organizations' processes and systems.
- Attention-based competencies involving management judgment / guidance may not scale as well or rapidly.

Parent firm should be as small as possible

Following the line of 'loosely joined' there is little reason to have a large center — and the last thing any organization wants is a significant share to fund 'corporate.'

There are certainly roles for the center (e.g., setting guidelines and managing the Information Architecture) and the center may develop capabilities (internally or with partners) that it makes available to the portfolio organizations.

But the emphasis here is on fostering portfolio organizations with the capability, drive and responsibility to make themselves successful.

Parent firms need to understand relative investment requirements and jump scales

It's possible that the parent within the IT Software & Services space might talk to the $2 billion IT cloud services organization today and a $50 million Retailer-in-a-cloud packaging organization tomorrow. Both bring strategic value to the enterprise (and one another) but work at very different scales.

Alphabet

The textbook case of a Portfolio Enterprise, Alphabet, emerged while I was writing this book — and it's helpful to view the Portfolio Enterprise through the lens of Google co-founder Larry Page's open letter announcing the change in August 2015 (quoted here at length):

> ... "Google is not a conventional company. We do not intend to become one." As part of that, we also said that you could expect us to make "smaller bets in areas that might seem very speculative or even strange when compared to our current businesses." From the start, we've always strived to do more, and to do important and meaningful things with the resources we have.
>
> We did a lot of things that seemed crazy at the time. Many of those crazy things now have over a billion users, like Google Maps, YouTube, Chrome, and Android. And we haven't

> stopped there. We are still trying to do things other people think are crazy but we are super excited about....
>
> Our company is operating well today, but we think we can make it cleaner and more accountable. So we are creating a new company, called Alphabet.... What is Alphabet? Alphabet is mostly a collection of companies. The largest of which, of course, is Google. This newer Google is a bit slimmed down, with the companies that are pretty far afield of our main internet products contained in Alphabet instead. What do we mean by far afield? Good examples are our health efforts: Life Sciences (that works on the glucose-sensing contact lens), and Calico (focused on longevity). Fundamentally, we believe this allows us more management scale, as we can run things independently that aren't very related.
>
> Alphabet is about businesses prospering through strong leaders and independence. In general, our model is to have a strong CEO who runs each business, with Sergey and me in service to them as needed. We will rigorously handle capital allocation and work to make sure each business is executing well. We'll also make sure we have a great CEO for each business, and we'll determine their compensation.... This new structure will allow us to keep tremendous focus on the extraordinary opportunities we have inside of Google.... Sergey and I are seriously in the business of starting new things.... We are also stoked about growing our investment arms, Ventures and Capital, as part of this new structure.

Note the deep language grounding Alphabet in purpose. Although the strategy is vague (Alphabet *née* Google has been about creating value out of data) this is about being what Google was always intended to be and striving to do big, important, and diverse things.

Much of what he articulates here is consistent with what I outlined earlier in the chapter: a portfolio of separate organizations, each with their own business objectives, linked with a center. The language here feels like a light center, but it is early days and we will see how that practically develops.

Finally (and critically), don't chalk this up to unconventional management practices in the Internet sector: for the reasons noted, the realities facing most every large established enterprise will warrant a similar approach (although maybe with less spread).

Close

Stepping back, the prescriptive takeaways for *Deliberate Performance* are:

- When an enterprise has competencies and outcomes that diverge — enterprises may need to consider an alternate operating concept — which I have referred to here as the Portfolio Enterprise.
- It is important that the value or purpose of the portfolio is understood as it drives the overall operating model at the enterprise level.

- *Loosely joined* principles are critical to strike the balance of creating value out of the portfolio but also ensuring that each organization owns its responsibility to succeed.

The structure balances a set of needs:

- *Organizations* receive resources, governance, and structure to focus on its business
- *Enterprises* obtain multiple avenues of growth and potential value-added opportunities from the set of organizations while minimizing potential disruptive conflicts
- *Stakeholders* (and management) gain transparency on value-add and returns.

Digression — Lily Pad Strategies

Back in Part II, I referred to lily pad strategies in yang tacticals. Having discussed Networked Competencies, yin-yang tactics within Strategic Objectives and portfolio enterprises, we are now better equipped to tackle the point further.

The Lily Pad approach is about leveraging the enterprise's or organization's current set of lily pads — assets in the form competencies, customers, or resources-processes-culture-innovation focus — to create or take advantage of a market opportunity.[23]

Take the case of our use case Integrated Financial Institution setting up a revamped retail personal financial management hub. From a yang tactical

---

[23] Lily Pad Strategies share common ground with pivoting in that they are both guided by current competencies, customers and/or resources-processes-culture-innovation focus.

Pivoting usually refers to changing the business model or value proposition of the organization — whereas Lily Pad strategies are more about growing the enterprise.

perspective, this is both an integrative value proposition — bringing together a suite of services and experience for the retail consumer — and subversion — in that you are attempting to subvert the experience expectation of the classic retail bank branch.

From the lily pad perspective, it leverages key assets of our Financial Institution, but establishes a different value proposition for our clients (factoring in the location and experience as part of the value proposition).

From an enterprise design point of view, to be successful — given there are significant fundamental differences in competencies / outcomes in this model — it needs to be executed and run in a separate, loosely joined organizational unit per guidelines in Part III and thus evolve towards a Portfolio Enterprise. Organizationally, you would most likely set this up as a distinct business unit and govern, test and launch the proposition as a start-up. Understand going in, the necessary alternate resources-processes-culture-innovation focus, be pragmatic about your enterprise's track record and ability to operate per loosely joined rules, and, zealously defend the loosely joined rules.

The Lily Pad approach, therefore, looks for points where market opportunity, current competencies, and brand largely overlap.

A few final points:

- As noted in Parts II and III, there is a cap as to how many lily pad opportunities one can undertake at a single time: each likely requires focused attention and capital — even if run separately. The cap will, of course, vary by enterprise and constituent organizations.
- The capability to operate as a portfolio enterprise is important to effectively support yin-yang tacticals. If an Entrant chooses an alternate approach or value proposition to the market, the Incumbent — given its core resources, processes, culture and innovation focus - needs the capability to defend. Or, for the use-case Integrated Financial Institution example above, it enables yang approaches while minimizing potential disruptive impact on core businesses.

PART IV - OPERATING STRATEGY - TACTICALS

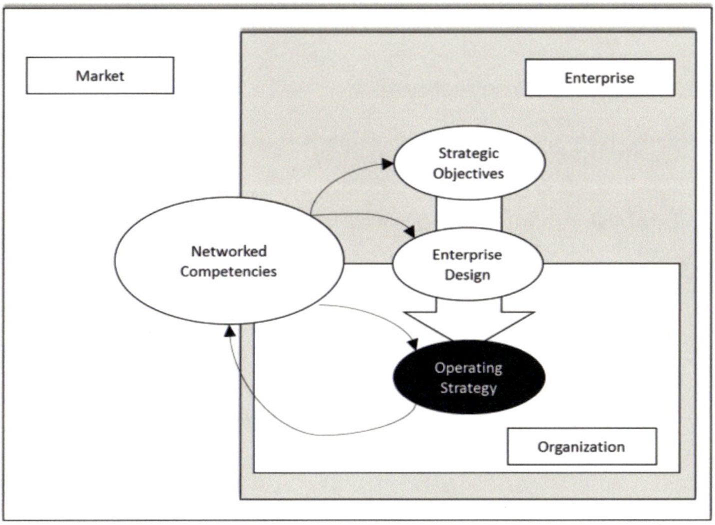

Much of the dialogue in ordinary course on Operating Strategy will be too specific to the organization and market to cover in this medium. The focus of *Deliberate Performance* method will be on tacticals within the organization and focusing particularly on clarity and responsiveness:

- Clarity — a clear, visible, shared, understanding of the organization's goals, process, roles / impact and data regarding external environment;
- Responsiveness — the ability, through culture, structure, process, systems, to identify and adapt as necessitated — or not — by changes.

Both contribute to developing a shared sense of purpose and creating a consistent framework upon which decisions are made — across the organization and aligned with the strategic objectives and targeted outcomes.

Part IV is broken into three sections:

- Clarify the Performance Narrative
- Establish the Information Architecture
- Engage the culture

Clarify the Performance Narrative. Purpose & Decisioning

The Performance Narrative aligns and actively connects employees with organizational objectives, using multiple angles to actively engage them.

This narrative is broken in four phases: Analysis, Implementation, Maintenance and Close / Renewal. The latter three make-up the Narrative Arc — a very explicit use of a (very human) storytelling framework — to focus the organization's efforts over a period of time.

Analysis

This phase is the groundwork to create the Narrative Arc, ie., developing the message.

Following the path of the book, you have distilled your market into a Networked Competencies view, worked through Strategic Objectives and, organizationally, determined how you intend to achieve those outcomes.

The objectives of the Performance Narrative are:

- Enunciate the organization's goals
- Understand everyone's connection to those goals, and
- State how they will be measured on it

The organization's goals will usually fall into several categories.

- Purpose (i.e., organization's reason for being);
- Some measure(s) of profitability (cash flow, earnings before interest and taxes, earnings before interest taxes depreciation and amortization, return on capital invested), which in itself emerges from

sales, direct variable cost, indirect overhead streams, days sales outstanding (how fast receivables are paid) and days payable outstanding how fast you're paying your bills);

- Stakeholder metrics (environmental metrics such as carbon footprint, health & safety);
- Shareholder value;
- Enterprise objectives (if organization is part of a broader entity).

In their “Primed to Perform,” ex-McKinsey consultants (now co-founders at Vega Factor) Neel Doshi and Lindsay McGregor highlight key leadership qualities driving total motivation of associates that they, in turn see driving high performance organizations:

Play

- Provides you with time, space, and encouragement to experiment and learn
- Makes it clear what it means to be performing well
- Challenges you to solve problems yourself

Purpose

- Helps you see that your work is important and meaningful
- Role models and expects to you live by positive, consistent values and a common sense of purpose
- Puts the customer’s interest first

Potential

- Actively links the work with your personal goals
- Helps you to develop and focus your time on your strengths rather than your weaknesses
- Provides you with more responsibility as your skills grow

Emotional Pressure

- Ensures targets and goals are fair and reasonable
- Is fair, honest and transparent
- Enables friendships at work

Economic Pressure

- Ensures you are evaluated holistically

Inertia

- Makes it easy to get things done and ensures you don't waste effort

I will return briefly to Total Motivation in Information Architecture as it relates to process design but the key takeaway for now is about reinforcing the importance of engaging the associate in purpose. Not every job needs to change the world directly, but it's fair to say most want to know they have an impact or make some kind of difference. The first step to harnessing individuals' performance is by them understanding the big picture and how their actions tie to those goals.

Understand how everyone in the organization — and the competency ring — contributes to those outcomes. These are great opportunities[24] for iterative discussions with front-line staff (and up) in operations, sales, IT, finance / accounting, HR, etc. as well as partners — so prepare properly.

Have a point of view on what measures progress towards achieving the objectives and key decision and behaviors that influence those metrics — but listen for links with other organization teams, their specific words (as those are breadcrumbs or fingerprints you can use when replaying), how they make decisions, and how they measure success.

Most importantly, continue tying back to purpose. Try different words — vary the narrative - to see what clicks.

Eventually (if you're using a white board & Sticky Notes) you will have something like the below.

---

[24] Some will hire consultants to do this work, but I strongly recommend involving organization's leadership in these discussions. Certainly a third party can facilitate and add structure but the benefits on engagement, credibility and management's appreciation of granular details are massive.

Sample Performance Model. One would go into the Activities at the consistent / relevant level of detail.

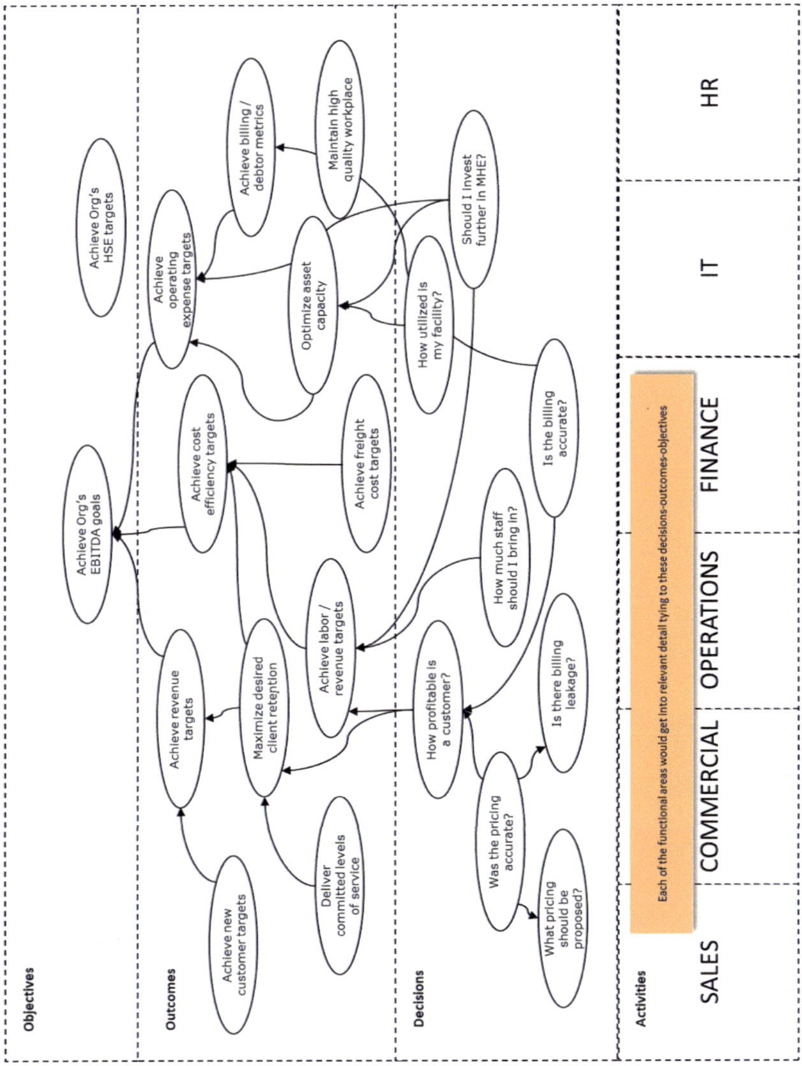

While it looks complex — when you break it down in smaller team discussions and follow narrative streams and talk to specifics, it can be a very effective tool to convey clarity and responsiveness — in particular to how decisions in one area affect another and how they impact the business. In presenting these models to functional teams, I will typically start with purpose and objectives then walk each activity / functional area up the page (activities -> decisions -> outcomes -> objectives) — and then put it all onto the board.

The last steps of analysis are typically informal discussions of the model — test it on small groups to see if you missed something, check wording, and sow a little anticipation. (When presenting to a group of varied associates, I usually start from objectives and work down through outcomes, decisions and activities.)

Narrative Arc — Implementation

Launching the Narrative Arc is straightforward enough, but a few points to consider in the communication:

- Set into the Bigger Picture. This phase takes place against a broader backdrop and you want associates mindful of same. "It will probably be a year or two … and achieving these objectives will allow us to …" Be clear about milestones.

- De-select. Juxtaposing what the organization is and what it isn't is critical (and potentially what's *really* important now vs not). There may be lots of ways to make money — and ideas to register — but attention is a scarce resource and you want the organization to focus on the stated objectives.
- Pace. Don't try and do too much too fast. As the organization leadership, you may have developed a view of what you want be and are primed to move and make needed decisions. But organizations — particularly larger ones — are constructs based on people and the rate of communication, absorption and change — particularly with larger organizations and changes that are more behavioral — will take time.
- Communicate core principles. Introduce 'rule of thumb' tools, memes, heuristics, and ear-worms (musical reference to a pop song sticking in your head) — to de-complicate decisioning. Streamlining your metrics of success — so a line manager has, say, three things to focus on for this period (using alert based IA tools to raise relevant exceptions) — is a start.

Narrative Arc — Maintenance

Sometimes staying the course is the hardest thing.

Particularly in larger organizations — where the time scales are longer — management will be faced with newly trending ideas: a changing market, evolving memes of the Next Big Thing, new ideas about how to succeed, etc.

And external stakeholders asking for a strategy regarding those newly trending ideas.

And the team may face internal stakeholders pressing for a set of shiny new initiatives with seemingly good returns on investment.

Pause though.

- Understand how those newly trending ideas fit into the plan. If customer relationships / interaction is central to the plan for our Financial Institution, then a social media strategy is important. It may be less relevant if the focus is on segmenting the development and servicing aspects of our IT Software & Services firm.
- Understand that not every good idea is worth doing now. By all means acknowledge a trend — even set-up a small group to analyze its impact

(Analysis for Next Arc) — but attention / focus is a scarce — and undervalued — resource.

Speaking from personal experience, it's easy to think incrementally ("This won't take too much time and shouldn't distract ... I am sure they'll have an hour here or there"), it's hard to argue against what appears to be an obvious good, and you don't want to discourage initiative.

- Maintain focus on the planned objectives. You believed — after discussing with your associates — that the plan was the right thing. Unless the new information fundamentally cuts at the core assumptions — consider the knock-on effects of not delivering. If the trending idea can somehow be — and authentically — incorporated, good. But even then, ensure language is about focusing on the original objective.
- Actively avoid initiative glut and the need to sound relevant: over-committing (likely already over-stretched) resources diminishes morale and both signal preference of image (saying 'yes' or sounding sexy) to substance.

Communicate regularly in formal updates (monthly / quarterly) to update on progress and informally in smaller groups — and get feedback.

Narrative Arc — Close / Renewal

Close will overlap with the Analysis and Renewal into the next phase (less the need to redo the Performance Model) but you want to explicitly close the current Arc while moving to the new one: speak to the accomplishments of the Arc and what worked (or didn't).

Maybe a little celebration — if you're so inclined — to punctuate.

Information Architecture

On one hand, I am surprised so much has been written about Big Data without getting into specifics regarding processes and cultural implications.[25]

---

[25] Although Part IV focuses on operational execution, it is worth a brief aside to highlight the potential opportunity to enhance customer value or branding through the information architecture.

Some of this was pointed out in the 'Leveraging the Network' portion of portfolio enterprises (customer interaction information and mining data for high transaction enterprises).

However, one could go further to connect the consumer dynamically with the product or its constituent components (e.g., communicating perhaps who designed the shirt, where/how it was made or, via immersive technologies, experience the design culture of a automobile manufacturer).

Information is obviously critical to improved decisioning so stating that organizations must have a suitable Information Architecture — by which I mean an aggregated view of data relevant to the organization – internal and external -- in an accessible way — should not surprise.

From a purely technical capability resources point of view, the news is good: next-gen service providers are out there extracting, normalizing, linking and interpreting data on scaling platforms, and, importantly, bringing costs down dramatically.

My focus in this section will therefore be on processes and values.

Remember throughout that the objective of the Information Architecture is to improve organizations' performance through decisions — which comes from access to information and the right processes and culture to leverage it.

Aesthetics and visualization are important but this is not exclusively about a rush to attractive dashboards.

Process

Granular, Simple & Transparent Structure

With the volume and breadth of data, granularity, simplicity and transparency should drive your architecture:

- Capture data elements at the most detailed granular level and add tags / attributes that align with other data sources and internal objectives.
- Add and/or normalize tags / data attributes as soon as possible and don't filter (except to get rid of bad data though even in that case I would suggest tagging it as bad) or change the data itself (unless you're certain it is incorrect or duplicate – in which case you would still likely want to systemically record same).
- If appropriate, have a standards document or set of filters for organizational — or firm — wide definitions (e.g., which transaction dates set the accounting period).

Like most things IT, most of the work is about upfront data quality so do not shortcut this process (nor let it drag on).

Incorporate Proliferating Data Trails

Data integration is no longer exclusively about linking internal systems and, I suspect, you will increasingly see industry focused ERPs and Business Intelligence platforms tapping those outside sources as well as core parts of their offerings.

Consider, too, the increased variations of data trails created by the 'internet of things': visibility to customers' arrival and movements within a store, soil conditions at a remote part of a farm, events in almost every corner of the world, aggregated pedestrian movements in NYC, location and functional history of large trucks nationwide, etc.

Consider also potential value of data sources: lead/lag socio-environmental indicators, related commodity prices, or activity in other areas in your Competency Network.

Design Process Workflow to Emphasize Decisions, Impactful Outcomes and Feedback

Process Workflow should be designed to minimize — and where possible eliminate — those tasks that consume attention on non-impactful outcomes and instead focus associates' valuable (and finite) time and attention to decisions and tasks with impactful outcomes. In Total Motivational [26] terms, this means designing the processes to afford and encourage decisioning and experimentation.

[26] Referred to back in the Performance Narrative section of Part IV

Information Architecture is not synonymous with process workflow — but their interaction points are critically important and they work very much hand-in-hand.

The Information Architecture should be designed to support those points of action by bringing requisite information at the appropriate time in the right form and context. It should also support innovation feedback loops, meaning (a) capture the actions taken, (b) tag those actions (A/B) in such a way to later glean which action may have yielded a better outcome and (c) include process / mechanism to review actions and outcomes.

(Information + Alignment) Replace Bureaucracies

If the direct win of good Information Architecture is enabling better / faster decisions, the indirect win is cutting out bureaucracies, tying individuals / teams closer to business outcomes (rather than isolated process outcomes) and replacing them with flatter structures supported by (rules and action-based) workflow and collaborative technologies.

Note: I am not justifying holacracy.[27] There are some core positives and environments of holacracy but I believe it has potential issues in judgment under uncertainty (some of which could be handled in IA but for anything unplanned) and resiliency (support structure and leadership when things go awry in unplanned fashion).

Several takeaways:

- Understand the processes and rules embedded in the workflow systems — are they consistent with your Operational Strategy and narrative about how decisions are distributed? A disconnect between practice and intent — unacknowledged and unaddressed — will fester and undermine the narrative.
- Use workflow tech aggressively to cut out bureaucracy, support appropriately distributed decision-making with relevant controls, decision support and feedback mechanisms. (On this point, I strongly

---

[27] From holacracy.org.

"Holacracy is a new way of running an organization that removes power from a management hierarchy and distributes it across clear roles, which can then be executed autonomously, without a micromanaging boss. The work is actually more structured than in a conventional company, just differently so. With Holacracy, there is a clear set of rules and processes for how a team breaks up its work, and defines its roles with clear responsibilities and expectations."

suggest executives take the time to deeply engage from the users' point of view during major systems implementations — and even potentially appoint a key role on the team — to ensure key values / objectives are incorporated).

- Understand and differentiate between decisions and ideas that require broader review and input (what Gore & Associates refer to 'below the waterline' — actions that can cause serious damage to the company) versus those than can be independently initiated.

Values

Underscore the Narrative

Whatever objectives are part of the Narrative Arc should be high visibility within the IA's presentation layer (i.e, dashboards, public video monitors).

Emphasize a data-based culture & skill set

Good, shared information enables — and needs — substantive conversations about correlations, sensitivities, lead / lag indicators, hypothesis development / testing, etc. in order to extract maximum value.

Hiring, training, and developing for these skill sets — again, in the context of targeted competency — is key.

Creating and encouraging opportunities for dialogue that scrutinizes and constructively talks to the data to extract implications and generates decisions / actions is important.

Emphasize the single collective source of truth

Single collective source of truth isn't intended to go Orwellian, but there needs to be an understanding that the information is factually The Truth.

That truth should stand up to rigorous and regular 'scientific' testing — meaning that if someone has reasonable belief that it may be wrong — test it. And if reasonable skepticism is expressed — test it.

But, testing aside, it's the source.

So if Bob says his data shows his revenues for his region were $1.5 million for the month versus the published $1.2 million, the difference should be understood — but the starting position is that $1.2 million is 'the number' given it is most consistently verifiable number — and that number should be the basis for action.

As an aside: rhythms are all over your business and the IA is no exception. While transactional systems are generally quasi real time, interpreting the data to make a decision usually requires some context — a threshold (e.g., error rate greater than 0.05%), a time frame (orders received by 8 PM), or a series of events (e.g., order placed v shipped v received) — to help give it meaning. Also — understanding and communicating the cadence and reporting time references is critical as updates / times can be a frequent source of confusion.

Visibility & Vulnerability

Understand, emotionally, what is going on.

If you are implementing a new IA into an organization or enterprise, you'll have the logical and semantic challenges of lining up definitions and relationships and you will experience the typical change-related obstacles common to system implementations.

The resulting information exposure also creates real visibility and vulnerability — for teams, staff and management — and potential risks to divert focus and attention.

For example, management may be amid a year where they want to focus on product growth initiatives, but other points emerge, thereby potentially diverting focus. For instance:

- Leadership of the western region (one of four) sees they generate 70% of the profits and bring up what you're going to do about it
- One of the regions is a huge drag on profits
- Two quarters into the year, top line revenue growth is negative year over year

All explainable and normal course but the increased visibility reduces management's ability to credibly control the dialogue. Management should prepare to lose some perceived control as associates are exposed to inconvenient information (realistically management should have dealt with these subjects anyway) and may have ideas / opinions on how to address (which ought to be considered).

Engage the Culture

In the Performance Narrative, I emphasized the importance of intense two-way communication and the Narrative Arc.

In discussing the IA, I underscored management's engagement in understanding the information platform (does it properly represent the Operating Strategy?) and the exposure it creates.

Much thus far in the organization is about clarity, shared purpose and transparency.

However, there needs to be an almost undermining undercurrent to prevent the organization from getting insular, dogmatic and rigid.

This is all about culture and management setting the tone and actively balancing the culture in order to maintain a pragmatic, open and dynamic organization.

There are several ways to address that, including:

- Embrace continuous improvement — if you can get better tomorrow, you are not perfect today ... which means you will err and you should assertively look for improvements, and create a safe place and culture for reasonable error.
- Intentionally create and use interactions (e.g., afforded in developing the Performance Narrative) to set the tone regarding how to unearth, discuss, clarify and work through differences.

- Question yourself publicly or speak to times when information influenced you to change your thinking. It's ok to change an opinion in light of new information (though don't be too fluid either ...) and use that as an opportunity to ground in root principles.
- Push back, constructively, on confidence and dogma.

Pitching humility and uncertainty with consistency of focus and narrative is, in the end, about balance and reminding and re-orienting the organization in the purpose and how to pragmatically achieve that purpose.

Digression — Transformation / Reinvention

Markets are moving rapidly and it's very possible to find your organization on the wrong side of a disruptive change or too far back of the competitive field.

Changing competencies becomes a real consideration as digging out of the hole you found yourself in takes attention, time and resource — and it's unlikely the competition hasn't set the bar higher in the meantime, thereby furthering the gap.

My language so far has been about either focusing an organization or adding / removing a business line or function. Transformation creates altogether different dynamics as you have to deconstruct and reconstruct the resources-processes-culture-innovation focus that are engrained in — and define — the organization.

It's cliché to say change is hard. Deceptively, rationally, it isn't. Twelve people can sit around a board room table and agree that a change is needed — but implementing structural, deep change is a very significant and extraordinary challenge. Here are some key points to consider when facing a potential transformation:

- The *Status Quo* has momentum — Associates, at all levels, will look to the past to predict the future: "we've done it in such-and-such-a-way for 40 years and we survived and thrived."
- The transformational strategic objective needs to *bridge* market need (outside-in) and as-is competencies / resources-processes-values (inside out). This book speaks repeatedly to the interplay of internal competencies and the market and the processes needed to successfully align strategic and operating decisions.
- The change will be highly emotional. The transformation narrative needs to invoke purpose, be *emotionally compelling* enough to overcome resistance, and should incorporate legacy values in some form. Do not assume that a rational framing of the problem (i.e., if we do not change, we will continue to fail and thus eventually lose our jobs) will result in the desired outcome.
- The objective needs to be *clear and distinctive*. Unless you can profitably execute at a next-gen like price reduction, simply copying a competitor's model makes for a risky strategy: internal and external

optics will suffer if the perception is you are moving opportunistically as a 'me too.'

- The objective should somehow *tie back* to legacy: from the end-consumer's perspective, why are you credibly better than a start up or than another established player?
- The process must be *comprehensive* touching all aspects discussed within this book.

There is no short-cutting — successful transformation will consume considerable time and attention. You will need to manage and monitor the transition through frequent interaction, gauge where the organization or teams are at on the cycle of change, and punctuate the position through communications pointing to data points — large and small.

MOVING FORWARD

This book followed four themes that underpin the *Deliberate Performance* method:

1. **Apply** Networked Competencies as an approach to understand markets, strategic objectives and operating strategies
2. **Distribute and align** decisions across the organization to drive performance through both a *narrative framework* and a robust *information architecture*
3. **Clarify purpose and strategic objectives and align** resources, processes, culture and innovation focus — all of which drive decisioning — accordingly to drive performance.
4. **Review, revisit, adjust** the enterprise's structure and enterprise-level resources, processes and culture in light of the new environment (particularly for incumbent enterprises).

The book is in sequential process order — from networked competencies' based market view to strategic objectives to enterprise design to operating strategy — so, you can literally proceed from front to back.

Questioning Current State

A selective approach could leverage processes or tenets within *Deliberate Performance* and identify key points requiring focus.

If you are going this route, get a broad swathe of views into and across the organization and remember also that the system is an "AND" function, not "OR." Failing in any of these items — in addition to the day-to-day execution and development of the business — will, over time, erode performance. Key questions to help select could include:

- Why does my organization exist? And to what extent is that understood by the organization and stakeholders?
- How is our market changing? How does our organization fit into the evolving marketplace?
- Have we identified key, differentiated, opportunities?
- What are we doing to develop our brand and communicate purpose?

- Have we identified potential threats? Is our enterprise or organization appropriate to counter it?
- Do we have a defined set of strategic objectives? Have we actively deselected potential options or initiatives?
- Is our organization / enterprise structurally designed to succeed - meaning do the key competencies within the company align with similar focus and outcome?
- Do we have the structure, resources, processes, culture to operate as a portfolio enterprise?
- Does everyone understand the purpose and strategic objectives of the organization - and how they contribute?
- Do our decisions and actions regarding what we do (i.e., resources-processes-culture-innovation) fit with our strategy / competency focus?
- How well do our information systems support timely and effective decision-making?
- How well do our information systems and processes support associate engagement? Do our processes afford time for our associates to experiment and engage?
- How much time do our leaders get to circulate and talk with associates?

Again, the objective here is to assess dynamics and prioritize / select key points — and you could certainly do this while you undertake the sequential process outlined herein.

Parting Words for Established Companies

Current mid- to large scale incumbent enterprises are, no doubt, challenged — and the answers are neither simple nor quick. But they require a deeper look at the enterprise's foundations:

- Recall the importance of purpose. This isn't about a vague Mission Statement that is approved because it either has a little for everyone or not offensive enough to generate opposition but rather an emotionally compelling idea that associates can engage with at either the enterprise or organizational level.
- Apply Networked Competencies to review the market you are in and where you fit. If you have multiple operating units, conduct the assessment on multiple units — is there an opportunity to reconfigure along competency lines? *How can you bring your associates closer to feeling ownership of the business outcomes of the operating units?*

- Assess your capability — or develop it — to operate multiple business units as a loosely joined portfolio enterprise. Odds are, in my view, it will be needed.
- Apply the Lily Pad approach to consider opportunities to leverage your as-is competencies.
- Is there an operating platform that can be wholesaled out — creating an econ-system out of the platform?
- Understand the value of the current portfolio organizations in the contexts of current performance, enterprise purpose, and intended strategic value(s) of the portfolio.

This naturally rolls into Enterprise Design (setting up a portfolio enterprise structure separating the constituent organizations) and Operating Tacticals (Performance Narrative, Information Architecture and Minding the Culture) already discussed.

Parting Words to 'Maturing' Organizations

A traditional stage of organizations 'maturing' has been an emphasis on processes, standardization and professionalism as they grow.

Take extreme care.

Your organization is a system requiring balance: introduce too much too fast and you risk diluting what made you special; introduce nothing and you risk being insular.

Know what made you great and, assuming that remains at your core, ensure it is constantly at center of decisions and priorities.

AFTERWARD

I am indebted to a slew of folk.

Professor Christian Harm - who bears the responsibility of introducing me to Ronald Coase.

Gordon Wright, Mike White and Bob Agresti for their professional and personal examples - smart, humble, generous and (bewilderingly) kind.

Britt Hurley, Jessica Drennan, Pat Peeke, Roger Phelps, Andrea DuCroiset, Joanna Scott, Jodie Patterson, Stephanie Klem, Pat Cook, Lauren McGarry, and Lorraine Davis for support and motivation.

Rob Petti, Laura Petti, Graham Scott, Bill Casswell, Debbie Carmody, and JR Geoffrion for support and also their time, attention and editorial support.

Leslie Winick for being there – ever enthusiastic and supportive - at the very beginning of the networked competencies journey and encouraging the first step in this book.

They should be credited for any value the book provides.

All errors lie with me. (And I hope I have not let any of you down.)

To my sons - Beck & Leo. Making me realize that, as a parent, I am indeed obligated to practice what I preach and take a risk.

Finally – to my wife, Irene. Encouraging. Challenging. Incredibly supportive. Putting up with this process (and particularly the time it took away from other, more practical, matters). Thank you so very, very much. There is no way this book could have been written without your words and patience.

ABOUT THE AUTHOR

Kai is a graduate from Cornell University, where he received his BA in Economics and from Stern School of Business (New York University), where he received his MBA in Economics and Finance.

He is currently the Executive Vice President of Information Technology and Warehouse Operations at O'Neill Logistics.

Kai lives in Martinsville NJ with his wife, Irene and two boys, Beck and Leo.

More information at www.folinomedia.com.

Made in the USA
Monee, IL
05 November 2026

67378294R00088